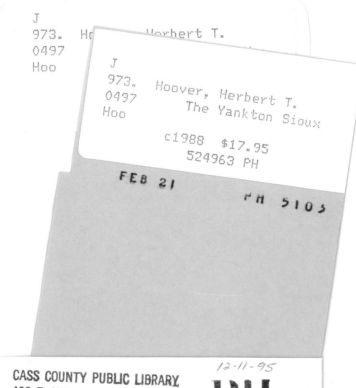

THE
YANKTON SIOUX

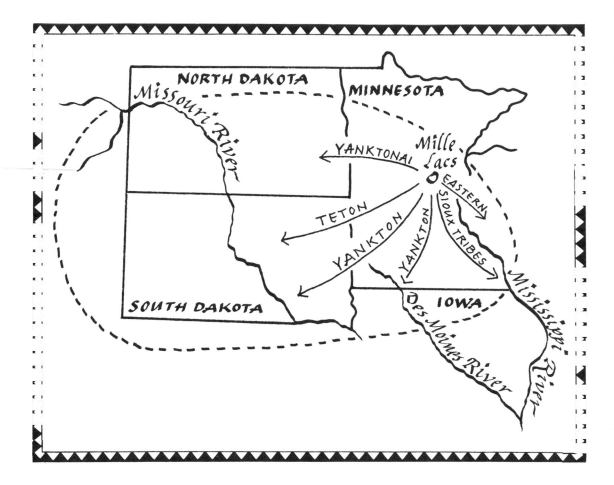

INDIANS OF NORTH AMERICA

THE YANKTON SIOUX

Herbert T. Hoover
University of South Dakota

in collaboration with
Leonard R. Bruguier

Frank W. Porter III
General Editor

CHELSEA HOUSE PUBLISHERS
New York   Philadelphia

On the cover A Yankton Sioux medicine circle of willow, yarn, feathers

Editor-in-Chief Nancy Toff
Executive Editor Remmel T. Nunn
Managing Editor Karyn Gullen Browne
Copy Chief Juliann Barbato
Picture Editor Adrian G. Allen
Art Director Giannella Garrett
Manufacturing Manager Gerald Levine

Staff for THE YANKTON SIOUX

Senior Editor Marjorie P. K. Weiser
Associate Editor Andrea E. Reynolds
Senior Designer Laurie Jewell
Design Assistant Laura Lang
Copy Editor Michael Goodman
Picture Research Ilene Cherna Bellovin
Production Coordinator Joe Romano

Creative Director Harold Steinberg

7 9 8 6

Library of Congress Cataloging in Publication Data

Hoover, Herbert T.
The Yankton Sioux.

(Indians of North America)
Bibliography: p.
Includes index.
Summary: Discusses the history of the Yankton Sioux
and their current situation. Includes a picture essay
on objects used in Yankton religious observance.
1. Yankton Indians—Juvenile literature.
[1. Yankton Indians. 2. Indians of North America]
I. Title. II. Series: Indians of North America
(Chelsea House Publishers)
E99.Y25H66 1988 973'.0497 87-18221

ISBN 1-55546-736-9
    0-7910-0369-8 (pbk.)

CONTENTS

INDIANS OF NORTH AMERICA

CHELSEA HOUSE PUBLISHERS

INDIANS OF NORTH AMERICA: CONFLICT AND SURVIVAL

Frank W. Porter III

*The Indians survived our
open intention of wiping them
out, and since the tide turned
they have even weathered
our good intentions toward them,
which can be much more deadly.*

John Steinbeck
America and Americans

When Europeans first reached the North American continent, they found hundreds of tribes occupying a vast and rich country. The newcomers quickly recognized the wealth of natural resources. They were not, however, so quick or willing to recognize the spiritual, cultural, and intellectual riches of the people they called Indians.

The Indians of North America examines the problems that develop when people with different cultures come together. For American Indians, the consequences of their interaction with non-Indian people have been both productive and tragic. The Europeans believed they had "discovered" a "New World," but their religious bigotry, cultural bias, and materialistic world view kept them from appreciating and understanding the people who lived in it. All too often they attempted to change the way of life of the indigenous people. The Spanish conquistadores wanted the Indians as a source of labor. The Christian missionaries, many of whom were English, viewed them as potential converts. French traders and trappers used the Indians as a means to obtain pelts. As Francis Parkman, the 19th-century historian, stated, "Spanish civilization crushed the Indian; English civilization scorned and neglected him; French civilization embraced and cherished him."

Nearly 500 years later, many people think of American Indians as curious vestiges of a distant past, waging a futile war to survive in a Space Age society. Even today, our understanding of the history and culture of American Indians is too often derived from unsympathetic, culturally biased, and inaccurate reports. The American Indian, described and portrayed in thousands of movies, television programs, books, articles, and government studies, has either been raised to the status of the "noble savage" or disparaged as the "wild Indian" who resisted the westward expansion of the American frontier.

Where in this popular view are the real Indians, the human beings and communities whose ancestors can be traced back to ice-age hunters? Where are the creative and indomitable people whose sophisticated technologies used the natural resources to ensure their survival, whose military skill might even have prevented European settlement of North America if not for devastating epidemics and the disruption of the ecology? Where are the men and women who are today diligently struggling to assert their legal rights and express once again the value of their heritage?

The various Indian tribes of North America, like people everywhere, have a history that includes population expansion, adaptation to a range of regional environments, trade across wide networks, internal strife, and warfare. This was the reality. Europeans justified their conquests, however, by creating a mythical image of the New World and its native people. In this myth, the New World was a virgin land, waiting for the Europeans. The arrival of Christopher Columbus ended a timeless primitiveness for the original inhabitants.

Also part of this myth was the debate over the origins of the American Indians. Fantastic and diverse answers were proposed by the early explorers, missionaries, and settlers. Some thought that the Indians were descended from the Ten Lost Tribes of Israel, others that they were descended from inhabitants of the lost continent of Atlantis. One writer suggested that the Indians had reached North America in another Noah's ark.

A later myth, perpetrated by many historians, focused on the relentless persecution during the past five centuries until only a scattering of these ''primitive'' people remained to be herded onto reservations. This view fails to chronicle the overt and covert ways in which the Indians successfully coped with the intruders.

All of these myths presented one-sided interpretations that ignored the complexity of European and American events and policies. All left serious questions unanswered. What were the origins of the American Indians? Where did they come from? How and when did they get to the New World? What was their life—their culture—really like?

In the late 1800s, anthropologists and archaeologists in the Smithsonian Institution's newly created Bureau of American Ethnology in Washington, D. C., began to study scientifically the history and culture of the Indians of North America. They were motivated by an honest belief that the Indians were on the verge of extinction and that along with them would vanish their languages, religious beliefs, technology, myths, and legends. These men and women went out to visit, study, and record data from as many Indian communities as possible before this information was forever lost.

8

By this time there was a new myth in the national consciousness. American Indians existed as figures in the American past. They had performed a historical mission. They had challenged white settlers who trekked across the continent. Once conquered, however, they were supposed to accept graciously the way of life of their conquerors.

The reality again was different. American Indians resisted both actively and passively. They refused to lose their unique identity, to be assimilated into white society. Many whites viewed the Indians not only as members of a conquered nation but also as "inferior" and "unequal." The rights of the Indians could be expanded, contracted, or modified as the conquerors saw fit. In every generation, white society asked itself what to do with the American Indians. Their answers have resulted in the twists and turns of federal Indian policy.

There were two general approaches. One way was to raise the Indians to a "higher level" by "civilizing" them. Zealous missionaries considered it their Christian duty to elevate the Indian through conversion and scanty education. The other approach was to ignore the Indians until they disappeared under pressure from the ever-expanding white society. The myth of the "vanishing Indian" gave stronger support to the latter option, helping to justify the taking of the Indians' land.

Prior to the end of the 18th century, there was no national policy on Indians simply because the American nation had not yet come into existence. American Indians similarly did not possess a political or social unity with which to confront the various Europeans. They were not homogeneous. Rather, they were loosely formed bands and tribes, speaking nearly 300 languages and thousands of dialects. The collective identity felt by Indians today is a result of their common experiences of defeat and/or mistreatment at the hands of whites.

During the colonial period, the British crown did not have a coordinated policy toward the Indians of North America. Specific tribes (most notably the Iroquois and the Cherokee) became military and political pawns used by both the crown and the individual colonies. The success of the American Revolution brought no immediate change. When the United States acquired new territory from France and Mexico in the early 19th century, the federal government wanted to open this land to settlement by homesteaders. But the Indian tribes that lived on this land had signed treaties with European governments assuring their title to the land. Now the United States assumed legal responsibility for honoring these treaties.

At first, President Thomas Jefferson believed that the Louisiana Purchase contained sufficient land for both the Indians and the white population.

Within a generation, though, it became clear that the Indians would not be allowed to remain. In the 1830s the federal government began to coerce the eastern tribes to sign treaties agreeing to relinquish their ancestral land and move west of the Mississippi River. Whenever these negotiations failed, President Andrew Jackson used the military to remove the Indians. The southeastern tribes, promised food and transportation during their removal to the West, were instead forced to walk the "Trail of Tears." More than 4,000 men, women, and children died during this forced march. The "removal policy" was successful in opening the land to homesteaders, but it created enormous hardships for the Indians.

By 1871 most of the tribes in the United States had signed treaties ceding most or all of their ancestral land in exchange for reservations and welfare. The treaty terms were intended to bind both parties for all time. But in the General Allotment Act of 1887, the federal government changed its policy again. Now the goal was to make tribal members into individual landowners and farmers, encouraging their absorption into white society. This policy was advantageous to whites who were eager to acquire Indian land, but it proved disastrous for the Indians. One hundred thirty-eight million acres of reservation land were subdivided into tracts of 160, 80, or as little as 40 acres, and allotted to tribe members on an individual basis. Land owned in this way was said to have "trust status" and could not be sold. But the surplus land—all Indian land not allotted to individuals— was opened (for sale) to white settlers. Ultimately, more than 90 million acres of land were taken from the Indians by legal and illegal means.

The resulting loss of land was a catastrophe for the Indians. It was necessary to make it illegal for Indians to sell their land to non-Indians. The Indian Reorganization Act of 1934 officially ended the allotment period. Tribes that voted to accept the provisions of this act were reorganized, and an effort was made to purchase land within preexisting reservations to restore an adequate land base.

Ten years later, in 1944, federal Indian policy again shifted. Now the federal government wanted to get out of the "Indian business." In 1953 an act of Congress named specific tribes whose trust status was to be ended "at the earliest possible time." This new law enabled the United States to end unilaterally, whether the Indians wished it or not, the special status that protected the land in Indian tribal reservations. In the 1950s federal Indian policy was to transfer federal responsibility and jurisdiction to state governments, encourage the physical relocation of Indian peoples from reservations to urban areas, and hasten the termination, or extinction, of tribes.

Between 1954 and 1962 Congress passed specific laws authorizing the termination of more than 100 tribal groups. The stated purpose of the termination policy was to ensure the full and complete integration of Indians into American society. However, there is a less benign way to interpret this legislation. Even as termination was being discussed in Congress, 133 separate bills were introduced to permit the transfer of trust land ownership from Indians to non-Indians.

With the Johnson administration in the 1960s the federal government began to reject termination. In the 1970s yet another Indian policy emerged. Known as "self-determination," it favored keeping the protective role of the federal government while increasing tribal participation in, and control of, important areas of local government. In 1983 President Reagan, in a policy statement on Indian affairs, restated the unique "government to government" relationship of the United States with the Indians. However, federal programs since then have moved toward transferring Indian affairs to individual states, which have long desired to gain control of Indian land and resources.

As long as American Indians retain power, land, and resources that are coveted by the states and the federal government, there will continue to be a "clash of cultures," and the issues will be contested in the courts, Congress, the White House, and even in the international human rights community. To give all Americans a greater comprehension of the issues and conflicts involving American Indians today is a major goal of this series. These issues are not easily understood, nor can these conflicts be readily resolved. The study of North American Indian history and culture is a necessary and important step toward that comprehension. All Americans must learn the history of the relations between the Indians and the federal government, recognize the unique legal status of the Indians, and understand the heritage and cultures of the Indians of North America.

Sioux families photographed near Fort Laramie, Wyoming, in the 1860s.

THE SIOUX
IN
AMERICAN HISTORY

The Sioux have been as important as any group of Indians in the history of the United States. Through their early years of contact with Europeans and white Americans, they were active in the fur trade, influential in dealing with federal officials, and helpful to explorers, missionaries, and other intruders. In the 1850s, they took up arms in self-defense against a wave of immigrants that trespassed on their land and threatened their culture. Since then, the Sioux have been at least as instrumental as any other tribe or federation of Native Americans in the development of federal Indian policy. They have been featured in literature and art, visible in entertainment media, and prominent in the image of American Indians held by peoples around the world.

The word *Sioux* is an abbreviation of a French term that was based on a word used by Ojibwa Indians. It meant *rattlesnake* and was used by the Ojibwas to identify the Sioux as their enemies. It has long been used in documents and literature, because no other term was coined to include all the people in the Sioux federation.

For centuries the Sioux attracted attention because there were so many of them. Their large population was divided into many tribes with the capacity to control a great deal of land. In the 17th century there were 25,000 or more, according to records left by French colonists from Quebec, who dealt with them in the upper Mississippi River valley region. In other words, approximately 1 of every 250 Indians in what is now the contiguous United States was Sioux.

Traders and missionaries believed at the time that there were only seven tribes, but they later learned that an eighth tribe of Sioux had moved to the western Canadian prairie before the French arrived. The names of the first seven were later spelled phonetically in English as Mdewakanton, Wahpekute, Sisseton, Wahpeton, Yankton, Yanktonai, and Teton. The eighth was the

13

Assiniboin (or Stony). Still later, the newcomers discovered that the Tetons consisted of seven tribes, whose names were written phonetically in English as Oglala, Brule, Minneconjou, Hunkpapa, Sans Arc, Two Kettle, and Blackfoot Sioux. Hence, the society known at first by non-Indians as a federation of 7 tribes was soon recognized as including 13 tribes in the United States and 1 in western Canada.

The French first found them camped in the summertime at permanent villages near Mille Lacs in east-central Minnesota. Here nearly all Sioux people (except the Assiniboin) lived in cabins made of poles and bark that had floor mats and porches added for comfort. Available around them were large beds of wild rice, lakes teeming with fish and birds, natural fruits and vegetables, woodlands containing small game, and plenty of room for gardening. The rest of the year they lived in portable tipis, which they carried with them when

they scattered to glean natural bounty in the winter months, and when they went on long expeditions south or westward to hunt big game during spring and fall. They lived and traveled together as members of related families formed into bands. Their leaders provided government and offered guidance in religion and philosophy. By the standards of that period in history, the Sioux lived in relative comfort. They were protected by lodges of soldiers, whose collective military strength was at least as great as that of any neighboring tribe or federation.

Traders from eastern Canada, however, favored the Ojibwas when they distributed European firearms. This placed the Sioux in jeopardy of attack by a better-armed enemy. To avoid a war with these neighbors, and to find better gleaning and hunting lands as well as trade connections to meet the needs of their growing population, Sioux people abandoned the cluster of

THE DIVISIONS OF THE SIOUX

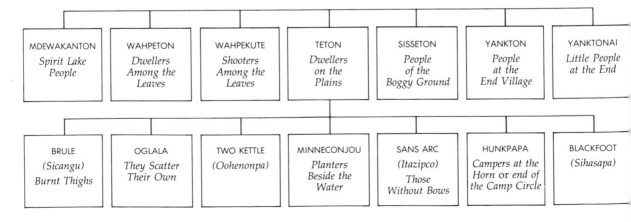

MDEWAKANTON	WAHPETON	WAHPEKUTE	TETON	SISSETON	YANKTON	YANKTONAI
Spirit Lake People	*Dwellers Among the Leaves*	*Shooters Among the Leaves*	*Dwellers on the Plains*	*People of the Boggy Ground*	*People at the End Village*	*Little People at the End*

BRULE	OGLALA	TWO KETTLE	MINNECONJOU	SANS ARC	HUNKPAPA	BLACKFOOT
(Sicangu) *Burnt Thighs*	*They Scatter Their Own*	*(Oohenonpa)*	*Planters Beside the Water*	*(Itazipco)* *Those Without Bows*	*Campers at the Horn or end of the Camp Circle*	*(Sihasapa)*

villages at Mille Lacs. By 1750, their tipi camps were spread out on areas marked by natural boundaries for their respective tribes. Their new territory stretched from the upper Mississippi River valley to the Black Hills region of what is now western South Dakota. They began to travel less widely on food-acquiring trips and generally stayed close to trading posts. By 1850, 13 Sioux tribes in the United States claimed by use or residence more than 80 million acres—an average of more than 2,500 acres for every member of the federation. Tetons generally lived west and the remainder east of the Missouri River, but Yanktons and Yanktonais retained hunting privileges on the plains and highlands surrounding the Black Hills.

Their territory gave the Sioux plenty of natural resources plus easy access to trade for surplus corn and vegetables grown by the Arikara whose villages were in the upper Missouri River valley. Across Sioux Country, the great northern buffalo herd grazed much of the time. Fur-bearing animals were plentiful as well. Merchants from almost every fur company that was active in the center of North America showed up at their camps to trade for the pelts and robes brought in by tribal hunters. Nor'west Company traders came from Montreal, Hudson's Bay Company merchants came down from farther north in Canada, and American Fur Company trappers and traders along with others traveled up from St. Louis and St. Charles in Missouri. In return

for hides and skins, the Sioux received trade goods that added comfort to life, and traps and guns that improved their efficiency in the chase for game. Bearing firearms on horseback, they became second to none on the hunt and awe-inspiring in defense of their territory. By 1850, the combined power of the Sioux soldiers' lodges was again easily a match for any other military force around them, including the army of the United States.

For 35 years and more, Sioux people used their power intermittently against non-Indians, as the smattering of welcome immigrants that provided trade goods grew into a hoard of land-hungry intruders that threatened their culture and invaded their land. Non-Indian habits and values began to replace Sioux traditions in the camps, as band members grew dependent on imported tobacco, coffee, sugar, salt, blankets, cloth goods, and manufactured articles of various kinds. Vice and crime undermined ancient moral standards where tribal members came in frequent contact with lawless adventurers, who lived in the settlements that sprang up to provide services needed for the increased steamboat transportation along the Mississippi and Missouri rivers. Christianity challenged ancient tribal beliefs and philosophies where missionaries introduced the teachings of Jesus. A wave of immigrant Norwegians and Germans flocked to the prairie of southern Minnesota. Gold seekers entered the Black Hills. Great caravans of wagons violated important hunting

In 1837 a visiting artist painted Sioux camped at the Fort Laramie trading post. The first battle fought by the United States against Plains Indians took place nearby in 1854.

ranges as they moved up the Platte River basin of Nebraska en route to Oregon, Utah, and California.

When the Sioux threatened war against the newcomers, federal officials met tribal leaders in areas of greatest danger to negotiate. In treaties signed at Mendota and Traverse des Sioux in 1851, the eastern Sioux surrendered claim to approximately 10 million acres across southern Minnesota and northern Iowa. In return, they accepted confinement to a narrow strip of land along the upper Minnesota River valley, together with the promise of yearly future payments in cash and supplies known as treaty annuities. In the Treaty of Fort Laramie the same year, Tetons, Yanktonais, and Yanktons offered safe pas-

sage to non-Indians migrating up the Platte River basin for the promise of future payments.

Diplomats on both sides worked earnestly to prevent a battle over land, but they could not stave off war for long. In 1854 hostilities broke out near Fort Laramie. This was the Grattan Affair, in which some Brules wiped out a military unit sent to make them pay for taking a lame cow that belonged to a Mormon immigrant. Quickly, General William Harney led federal troops in retaliation at the Battle of Ash Hollow, then displayed the growing strength of the U.S. Army by founding Fort Randall deep in Sioux Country. In 1857, Wahpekute Sioux soldiers under band leader Inkpaduta boldly attacked pioneers of northwestern Iowa in the Spirit Lake Massacre. They terrorized settlers of southern Minnesota near present-day Jackson along the upper Des Moines River valley. Minnesota militia chased Inkpaduta's raiders out of the area, but in 1862, in the Minnesota Sioux War, many Mdewakantons, Wahpekutes, Sissetons, and fewer Wahpetons followed Chief Little Crow in attack with such force that more than 25,000 non-Indians fled eastward to safety. Nearly 600 non-Indians and several hundred Indians were killed. From the mid-1860s to the late 1870s, Tetons and Yanktonais joined neighboring Indians west of the Missouri River in the wars led by Red Cloud and Sitting Bull to drive out all non-Indians except those who brought trade goods and annuities. For more than 20 years Sioux military forces stood their ground.

By the 1860s, settlers from the East occupied more and more Indian land. To defend their property, Sioux led by Little Crow killed some 600 settlers. These survivors were photographed after fleeing with whatever possessions they could salvage.

Gradually, however, non-Indians gained military superiority through the force of numbers backed by industrial support and efficient transportation. The outcome was apparent by the late 1870s. The Sioux wars came to an end in 1890 with the assassination of Sitting Bull on the Grand River, and the killing of many of his followers at Wounded Knee near Pine Ridge, in an attack by the U.S. Cavalry.

At every opportunity opened by victory in battle, treaty, or congressional agreement, non-Indian farmers, cattlemen, miners, merchants, and others moved into the war zone. Their arrival had dramatic effects. One was a reversal in racial attitudes. Many Sioux people, who had learned to live next to their selfish but useful non-Indian neighbors, now came to resent them deeply as callous intruders without respect for Indian land claims or cultural values. The new arrivals had come West at the invitation of politicians and business leaders, believing that Indians were the noble creatures depicted in European and American literature. Now these newcomers grew to think of the Indians as aggressive, inhuman warriors. The racism that emerged through the war years of the 19th century has abated somewhat over time, but it remains a force as strong in Sioux Country as in any other part of the United States a century later.

Another consequence of warfare and cultural conflict was popular demand for the rigorous application of federal Indian policies that had evolved

to deal with Indians who resisted the expansion of Anglo-American society. From the time of early conflicts between Indians and settlers in colonial Virginia, non-Indian officials had often attempted to segregate tribal groups on reservations in order to open land for settlement by non-Indians. They also used educational methods to prepare Indians for entry into mainstream society as citizens. Colonial leaders defended the morality of taking Indian land with the argument that the world contained a limited amount of land suitable for agriculture, and that those who could use it well in food production were entitled to seize it from those who could not—by force if necessary. They claimed legal authority to interfere in the lives of Indians through beliefs that the regional sovereignty of tribes was inferior to the imperial sovereignty of European kings, and the triumph of white over Indian culture was ordained by God.

Leaders in the Congress of the United States inherited these colonial assumptions and used them as bases for federal Indian policies. Drawing authority from the Constitution, they wrote laws that declared Indian Country to be a place apart from land occupied by other Americans. Indians should live as tribes in segregation until they could integrate with non-Indians and become individual U.S. citizens. An act of Congress in 1819 provided initial funding to support the formal education of Indians, using methods designed to hasten the replacement

Settlers in Indian Country lived at a distance from one another and saw each other only when attending church services, raising a barn, or completing a quilt.

tribal ways. Indians were pressured to adopt the same habits and beliefs that were being imposed on immigrants who applied for citizenship in the cultural melting pot of the United States.

Under these policies, Indians who retained their attachments to tribes were segregated geographically from other Americans. Federal officials alone had authority to govern their dealings with non-Indians—supervising all commercial as well as official contacts—or to acquire portions of land in Indian Country by treaties. Non-Indians had to get permission from federal officials to go into Indian Country. This was to protect the Indians and their territory from being overrun by land-hungry non-Indians. Federal leaders expressed in many ways their intention eventually to eliminate tribes as legal or cultural entities by gradually integrating their members into mainstream society. Voters encouraged the use of public funds to bring this about. Forced *acculturation* (getting tribal members to adopt non-Indian behavior and customs) was preferable to bloodshed over land, and it seemed inevitable with the growth of mainstream society.

Yet wars broke out in areas west of the Mississippi River where land was coveted most by non-Indians and tribes were strong enough to challenge intruders. Nowhere in the West did non-Indians exert greater pressure to occupy Indian Country than on the 80 million acres controlled by Sioux. Nowhere in the West were Indians better able to take up arms in defense of their land and culture than here.

Twelve of 13 Sioux tribes participated officially in their federation's intermittent resistance for 36 years. The wars cost dearly in funds, materials, bloodshed, racial attitudes, and freedom for Indians. When they ended, the 13 Sioux tribes of the United States were scattered among 27 locations in 5 states and 2 Canadian provinces.

The four tribes of Minnesota Sioux now occupied five small areas in southern Minnesota, one reservation in Nebraska, two in South Dakota, one in North Dakota, one in Montana, and (for those driven into exile by the Minnesota Sioux War) seven reserves in Manitoba and Saskatchewan. The seven tribes of Tetons settled with Yanktonais on six reservations in South and North Dakota, one reserve in Montana, and three small tracts of land at isolated locations on defensible highlands in western Canada.

Nearly everything changed for Sioux people in the United States during the war years except their relationship to federal officials and their firm determination to somehow keep an ancient culture intact. The situation in Canada was about the same, for the two countries had evolved from the same British Empire to develop similar attitudes and policies toward Native Americans. On both sides of the border, national governments asserted their sovereignty over tribes and placed them under the protection of national officials. Both governments claimed sole rights to control the relationships of Sioux with non-Indians and to administer efforts to change the cultural habits of tribal members.

Some acculturation efforts were already in use. During the second quarter of the 19th century, Congress allocated funds for hiring Christian missionaries to educate Sioux children at day schools and to introduce Anglo-American habits along with Christian beliefs among adults. Congress paid federal employees, known as U.S. farmers, to show family heads how to improve gardening techniques already in use part-time, hoping they would become self-sufficient food producers on family farms, like non-Indians. Government employees distributed corn, hoes, oxen, and plows to encourage agriculture. Federal officials restricted the geographic movement of the Sioux by assigning the various bands to specific trading posts and distributing annuities at designated places.

As one Sioux tribe after another gave up its arms and ponies to accept reservation life during the war years, acculturation tactics became more elaborate. Hundreds of federal employees joined reservation work forces that varied according to the sizes of tribes and their degrees of resistance to change.

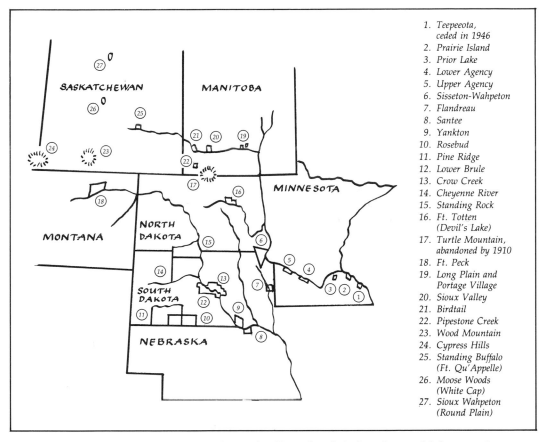

1. Teepeeota,
   ceded in 1946
2. Prairie Island
3. Prior Lake
4. Lower Agency
5. Upper Agency
6. Sisseton-Wahpeton
7. Flandreau
8. Santee
9. Yankton
10. Rosebud
11. Pine Ridge
12. Lower Brule
13. Crow Creek
14. Cheyenne River
15. Standing Rock
16. Ft. Totten
    (Devil's Lake)
17. Turtle Mountain,
    abandoned by 1910
18. Ft. Peck
19. Long Plain and
    Portage Village
20. Sioux Valley
21. Birdtail
22. Pipestone Creek
23. Wood Mountain
24. Cypress Hills
25. Standing Buffalo
    (Ft. Qu'Appelle)
26. Moose Woods
    (White Cap)
27. Sioux Wahpeton
    (Round Plain)

Sites numbered 17, 23, and 24 were chosen by Sioux for their location on high ground.

On average, the staff at an agency in Sioux Country included the agent, a clerk, one or two assistant clerks, an issue clerk to hand out annuities and gratuities, a physician, several U.S. farmers, many teachers, some resident missionaries, carpenters and blacksmiths, a cattle herder or two, some teamsters, a force of tribal police, a few Indian judges, several laborers, and many who worked around the agency part-time. Later came field matrons, nurses, and other agency personnel.

From the 1850s to the 1930s, thousands of people, both Indians and non-Indians, drew salaries from public funds and tribal annuities to manage affairs among Indians segregated on the reservations of the Sioux, and to bring individual Indians out of tribal life into mainstream society.

Today the procedures developed from the 1850s to the 1930s are somewhat altered, but the central goal of federal policy toward Indians remains the same. Under pressure from non-Indians in the area, federal employees continue to work among those Sioux people who prefer to live part- or full-time on reservations in tribal environments. The federal workers protect the reservation's inhabitants from geographic or legal intrusions by non-Indians. Yet many continue to encourage Indians to become integrated with other Americans, at the expense and eventual destruction of their tribal traditions.

For more than 150 years, officials of the United States have worked among Sioux people in the belief that at some time in the history of each tribe its members would become self-sufficient. Federal responsibility for them would end. Recently the term *self-determination* has been used to imply that this time is near for most tribes. The word *termination* has been used to acknowledge the advancement of a tribe to a point where federal protection and support has become unnecessary, and the tribe has either ceased to exist or assumed entire responsibility for its own members.

These terms express the continuing policies of the United States regarding Indians, policies that originated in colonial times. No one example can illustrate every aspect of their application in Sioux Country. The experiences of the larger Sioux tribes that have substantial amounts of land show best how groups in isolation have retained Indian ways in defiance of efforts by outsiders to change them. The histories of the smaller tribes with little land reveal how scattered groups with continual exposure to non-Indians have had the great-est struggle in resistance. The histories of those tribes with midsize populations and reservation areas present a blend of the two extremes and the greatest variety of experience.

The history of Yanktons is one of the best illustrations of varied relations with non-Indians. The size of their population has been close to average among the tribes of the Sioux federation. Their reservation, long located near the geographic center of Sioux Country, has been large enough to sustain a traditional way of life, yet small enough to subject its residents to frequent contact with non-Indians. During the Indian Wars, Yanktons stood alone among Sioux in their refusal to take up arms officially against the United States. For this reason, they have had an uninterrupted working relationship with federal officials reaching back further in time than that of any other Sioux tribe. Their agency is the oldest. Their reservation contains buildings and institutions of acculturation established earlier than those of any other tribe of Sioux. Aside from military involvement, their history provides the best general expression of life experienced by all Sioux people throughout the history of their relationships with federal officials and other non-Indians. The circumstances of the Yankton today are representative of those of all other tribes in the Sioux federation.

This book focuses on the Yankton past, but it is about major developments in the history of the entire Sioux federation. Where the illustrations

A typical Yankton tipi camp of the early reservation years. As long as the surrounding countryside was not heavily populated, Sioux bands could go off the reservation to hunt and gather food.

show other Sioux tribes, they represent developments in Yankton history about which no photographs are preserved in files available for general use. In each case, the facility or development rep-

resented is of the same kind as one described in historical records about the Yankton tribe. In all such cases, appropriate identification is included in the caption. ▲

Peter Longfoot was the son of Chief War Eagle. As a scout under General Alfred Sully, he tried to keep peace between Indians and non-Indians along the James River basin. Longfoot lived until 1916. His Yankton descendants today include "War" in their names as a memento of this proud heritage.

THE
YANKTONS
BEFORE 1859

The first reference in history to the Yanktons was on a map made during the 1680s. In 1700, the French trader-explorer Pierre Charles Le Sueur identified them as "Hinhanetons" at the "village of the red-stone quarry," near the headwaters of the Des Moines River in southwestern Minnesota. (A more accurate pronunciation of their own name for themselves would have been *Ee hank ton' u wans*.) All the Sioux considered this quarry a holy place and came to it often to mine the special stone they used to make Sacred Pipes. In their traditional religion, they contacted the Supreme Being *Wakantanka Tunkasina* by means of the Pipe, just as Christian believers prayed to God through the person of Jesus as the intercessor. At this holy place, Sioux people left offerings with prayers at the Three Maidens Rocks and held ceremonies in sweatlodges to ask the Great Spirit for permission to dig for pipestone. Then they quarried stone and carved Pipes for use in daily worship or special ceremonies.

Like other Sioux, Yanktons went to the quarry often for stone and could have been at the site for that purpose when Le Sueur met them in the year 1700; or the Yanktons might have been near the Pipestone Quarry because it was situated along a corridor of land they used while on the hunt or to travel to the Black Hills region. When they lived near Mille Lacs, Yanktons moved through the area at least twice a year on food-getting expeditions.

About half a century after Le Sueur encountered them, they left Mille Lacs to live in scattered villages on prairie land that they had long used for gleaning and hunting. Yanktons claimed approximately 13.5 million acres between the upper Des Moines and Missouri river valleys—more than 6,000 acres per member of their tribe. Although they used the entire region for gathering and hunting food, they lived most of the time in the tipi villages of seven bands scattered along the north bank of the Missouri River, upstream from the mouth of the Big Sioux.

"The Red Pipe-Stone Quarry of the Great Spirit," sketched by the artist George Catlin, where the Sioux mined the stone used to make their Sacred Pipes. The stone is now called catlinite.

This is where non-Indians began to deal with them regularly, late in the 18th century. At the lower James River basin, French trader Pierre Dorion settled in a tipi with a Yankton wife to raise a family of mixed heritage. West of the band villages, St. Louis merchant Jean Baptiste Trudeau built the first trading post used by the Sioux since they left Mille Lacs. At several tipi villages in this area, explorers Meriwether Lewis and William Clark made official contact with Sioux leaders on behalf of the United States. Upstream in 1812, St. Louis trader Manuel Lisa opened the first federal agency in Sioux Country, and lived there part-time as the first U.S. sub-agent to serve among Indians of the upper Missouri River drainage basin.

As long as fur traders were more numerous than other non-Indians in the region, the territory claimed by the

Yanktons was on the front line of contact between the Sioux and newcomers. From the time of Trudeau's arrival, Yanktons were the first to meet passengers on riverboats moving up the Missouri River. In the mid-1820s, they joined the U.S. Army's attack on the Arikaras. In 1830 they became the first Sioux to give up a large tract of land; by a treaty at Prairie du Chien, they ceded 2.2 million acres to the United States to ease tension in the region by keeping the tribes separated. By that time, St. Louis merchants were operating more trading posts and forts on land controlled by Yanktons than on any other area held by another tribe in the Missouri River drainage basin. Around the edges of Yankton Country, there were small posts near Lake Traverse, in Brown's Valley, and at Lac qui Parle along the upper Minnesota River; on the upper Des Moines River valley; along the north bank of the Missouri River at Running Water; and near the mouth of the Big Sioux River. Close to all their villages were two major trading centers: Fort Vermillion, located on land controlled by band chief Mad Bull, near the center of the encampments, and Fort Pierre, where the Bad River entered the Missouri to the northwest.

Fort Pierre, founded as the trading post Fort Tecumseh in 1823, became a major commercial center. Pierre Chouteau, Jr., who ran it after 1827, renamed it for himself. The present capital of South Dakota was established as East Pierre across the Missouri River from the fort.

INTRUSION OF NON-INDIANS IN THE 1850S

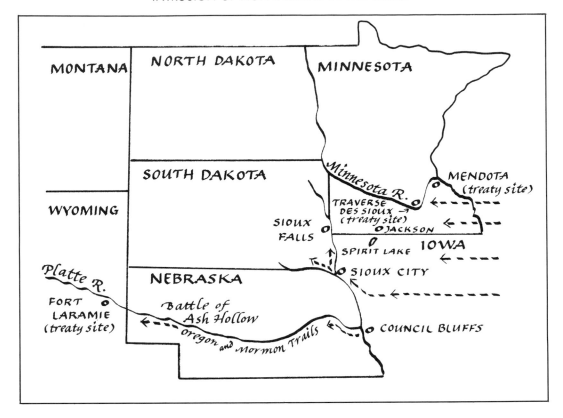

In exchange for furs and hides, traders offered blankets, cloth goods, manufactured clothing, trinkets, household wares, tools, colorful beads for use in arts and paraphernalia, and the best firearms and accessories available to kill game of all sizes for their skins. Pierre Chouteau, Jr., the leading trader at St. Louis, ran the first fleet of steamboats past Yankton villages to carry on this trade. Chouteau also transported the supplies purchased by the United States from his warehouses for distribution as annuities and presents among Indians. Chouteau's boats brought many passengers from the East, including artists George Catlin and Karl Bod-

mer, ornithologist John Audubon, and Jesuit missionary Pierre Jean De Smet. Yanktons mingled and intermarried with traders as they dealt with a steady stream of visitors until the middle of the 19th century.

The visitors spread the word that Yanktons were peaceable people. They described the Yankton Delta, or Triangle, between the Big Sioux and Missouri rivers, as one of the best locations for agriculture in the West. This was welcome news to tens of thousands seeking refuge on American frontiers.

After midcentury came a rush of immigrants from abroad. Political and economic troubles drove millions out of

Europe into exile on frontiers in Latin America, Australia, and Canada as well as in the western United States. Immigrants crossed the Mississippi River in ever-increasing numbers after 1850 to mine gold and silver, work as ox-cart drivers or at wood stations to supply fuel for steamboat transportation, take jobs in military units or Indian agencies, sell livestock, build towns and cities, and settle on farmland offered at low cost by the U.S. government as rapidly as it was ceded by Indian treaties.

Into Sioux Country came federal employees, transportation workers, and town builders, followed by a hoard in search of land for farming. At the east end of the Yankton Triangle, Sioux Falls and Sioux City sprang up in the mid-1850s. On unfarmed land claimed by Yanktons, settlers squatted (settled illegally) to await its purchase by federal officials and survey for sale to farmers.

The Department of the Interior was the federal agency concerned with Indians through its Bureau of Indian Af-

PRINCIPAL PLACES OF FUR TRADE AND
YANKTON BAND VILLAGE SITES, 1823–1859

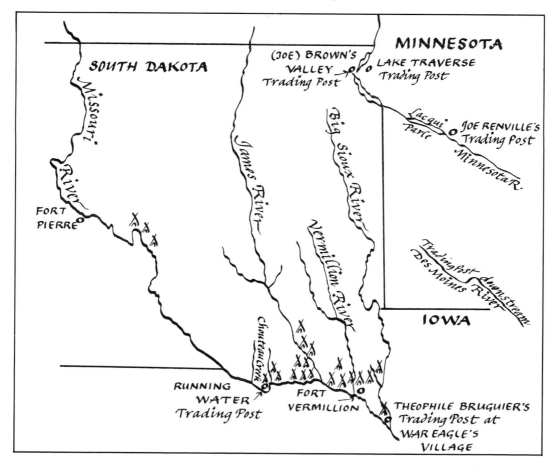

fairs (BIA). Under pressure from politicians and real estate agents, the secretary of the interior called for the removal of Yanktons from their fertile Triangle to a small reservation in the Missouri Hills. Tribal leaders had to decide whether to join other Sioux in armed resistance against American officials and settlers, or to make room for immigrants and live beside them in peace. More than 50 years of almost continuous and mutually beneficial contact with non-Indians influenced their choice of peaceful coexistence. Head Chief Struck-by-the-Ree led other tribal leaders to the national capital where, in the Treaty of Washington in 1858, they gave up 11,155,890 acres on the Triangle. All that remained of their vast territory was a section of land containing the Pipestone Quarry and a new reservation comprising 430,000 acres in the Missouri Hills west of Chouteau Creek. In all, Yanktons gave up more than 5,000 acres per tribal member in return for some 200 per member. As compensation for this loss, they were promised $1.6 million to be paid in annuities and services over 50 years, along with an agency to be established on

Dress worn by a Yankton woman, made of buckskin with beaded trim.

An Assiniboin woman and girl, sketched by George Catlin during his travels in Sioux Country.

Sioux use a cable ferry to cross the flood-swollen North Platte River. This photograph was taken near Fort Laramie during the Treaty Council meeting of 1868.

their reservation. At the agency, federal employees would help them adjust to family farming and ranching and in other ways prepare them for U.S. citizenship.

As the first installment of annuity supplies arrived on the steamboat *Carrier* in the summer of 1859, Yanktons began to pull up stakes at their tipi villages. Traveling overland, they approached the new Yankton Agency. The agency was soon named Greenwood for the U.S. commissioner of Indian affairs who was in charge as the Yankton people assembled on the new reservation. ▲

Head Chief Struck-by-the-Ree was photographed when he led a delegation of tribal leaders to Washington. In 1858 they signed a treaty that gave them a reservation of 430,000 acres and annual payments but they relinquished a far larger tract of land. "Old Strike" led the Yanktons in peaceable accommodation to change.

ADJUSTING
TO
NON-INDIAN WAYS

Greenwood Agency grew quickly into a bustling town. Along Main Street, there were agency headquarters, some housing for federal employees, two missions, a few general stores run by merchants with federal licenses, and a livery stable. On a parallel street near the river, there were warehouses to store annuity goods and agency supplies and a three-story hotel used by visitors who came to do business there or make connections for travel elsewhere. This busy section was known as Mile Square, because it centered on the square mile of land on which the agency was located.

Greenwood Agency served as the hub in a network of transportation routes. There was a docking place for steamboats on the riverbank. A ferry crossed the Missouri to Nebraska at the mouth of Mosquito Creek, a quarter of a mile downstream. Greenwood was a station on the military road from Sioux City to Fort Randall, over which scheduled stagecoaches traveled carrying

passengers, mail, and light cargo. This military road followed an old Indian trail, which came up the north bank of the Missouri and merged with other trails about 15 miles north of Greenwood. From the crossroad, one trail ran toward Minnesota in the east, another along the Missouri Hills to the northwest, and a third into the Black Hills region across the Missouri at the ford below a landmark called The Tower. After Greenwood was established, old trails became wagon roads, and Yanktons were exposed daily to non-Indian travelers.

More than that, they were exposed to the first permanent agency staff to serve in Sioux Country. Drawing special allocations from Congress as well as funds provided by the 1858 treaty, the issue clerk handed out supplies and cash to chiefs for distribution among family heads to prevent starvation and suffering. The agent set up a tribal police force to maintain order and talked with chiefs about the proper use of cer-

The Yankton reservation had magnificent scenery and was ideal for religious ceremonies. Wood, water, and game were plentiful, but the land was poorly suited to agriculture.

tain treaty funds. On their advice, he created an eighth band for tribal members of mixed Indian-white heritage and named Francis Deloria its chief. The staff at Greenwood hired laborers to break ground for farming and build a mill at the edge of town to prepare lumber. Workers began construction on agency facilities. A carpenter, a blacksmith, and a tinsmith taught Yankton men how to build new homes and maintain their agricultural equipment. Teachers went on the payroll to operate a day school for youngsters.

Meanwhile, the tribe was busy with its own agenda under Head Chief Struck-by-the-Ree. As the *Carrier* unloaded supplies at the Yankton agency in the summer of 1859, he arrived at a site in the Missouri Hills with an advance party of several hundred. Standing on a shelf of land remembered as The End of the Trail, about a mile downstream from Greenwood, he called for his Pipe. Old Strike, as he was sometimes called, prayed to the four directions (west, north, east, and south) and then up (to Wakantanka) and down (to Mother Earth) in the traditional way. He told the Yankton people that they should follow a course of cooperation and acceptance. They must gather on the reservation, stay at peace, and reject appeals from other Sioux tribes for help in war against non-Indians.

The head chief's pronouncement has been commemorated in several ways. It was reenacted at The End of the Trail by elders in the 1920s. Participants requested that they be buried at the site, and it was marked as a place of special importance in tribal history by depressions over their graves. Old Strike's leadership in peaceable adjustment is remembered by the Yankton Sioux Monument, placed on the bluff overlooking Greenwood at tribal expense, on which are inscribed the names of those who negotiated the treaty of 1858.

From the place called The End of the Trail, band groups spread out along the southern and western edges of the reservation, where they had access to wood and water, hunting and fishing, and protection against harsh weather during the winter months. Yanktons grouped in tipi camps by bands, following approximately the same geographic arrangement they had used on the Tri-

angle. Mad Bull's people were still on the front line of exposure to non-Indians at a village near the place where Chouteau Creek ran into the Missouri River. Band groups represented by Struck-by-the-Ree, White Swan, and one or two of the other chiefs most willing to accept federal policies set up villages in the Missouri valley close to Greenwood. Those traditionalists who resisted change became the "upper bands." They kept their distance from non-Indians, spoke out against federal policies freely, and stayed in touch with Tetons and Yanktonais who fought in the wars of Red Cloud and Sitting Bull.

From the eight villages, families moved about on the reservation to gather wild fruit, vegetables, migratory birds' eggs, and other natural bounty. When there was not enough food on the reservation, hunting parties crossed

Main Street in Greenwood, the site of the Yankton reservation agency, was a commercial center. At left, horses are tied up near the livery stable. There are a blacksmith shop, two trading posts, and a barbershop on the street.

the Missouri to look for buffalo, and the agents sent wagons out to haul in the meat. Small bands continued to hunt and gather food on the Triangle west of the James River. At least twice a month, each band assembled at Greenwood for issue days, when supplies were given out by the agency. After 1870, a head of household drew for every family member a portion of beef, flour, sugar, salt, coffee, tobacco, soap, clothing, and more. Whenever a matter of vital importance justified an assembly of the general council of tribal adults, Yanktons gathered in a massive tipi camp that blanketed the hillside and breaks above Greenwood.

To outsiders, reservation existence through the 1860s may have seemed like traditional life confined in a small space. Agency employees were at work to make it otherwise, however, as quickly as they could. No item on their agenda seemed more urgent than the order to move Yankton people from their band villages into permanent housing on scattered family farms. Tipis would be replaced by log cabins on rectangular plots of communal land assigned to family heads. The goal was to encourage farming as the main way of life and replace dependence on shared tribal natural resources with free enterprise. In addition, the change would separate band members from each other enough to discourage participation in such traditional activities as dances, give-aways, and religious ceremonies.

Give-aways were festive gatherings sponsored by some person or group to honor an individual on a special occasion. The occasion might be a birthday, a naming, a memorial for someone who had died, or some other event of traditional significance. The sponsor provided a lavish feast and distributed to all guests gifts of monetary, practical, or cultural value. Gifts with the greatest meaning would go to those people who were most closely associated with the person being honored by the give-away. Sponsors might give away agricultural equipment, food, and clothing received as annuity goods or wages earned by their labor. Give-aways expressed a key cultural value of the Sioux—sharing. Often a sponsor was reciprocating for honors or gifts previously received. Federal officials were particularly eager to suppress give-aways because the sharing of property in this way was so contrary to the principles of capitalism that they were trying to instill in the Indians. Give-aways prevented the Sioux from storing food and saving money for the future.

Greenwood agents hired Yankton family heads to do part-time construction work on round-log cabins at farmsites. Funds had been allocated by Congress for this purpose. Yankton wives, children, and other relatives were to live in the log cabins. The agency employee known as a U.S. farmer traveled among them to show how non-Indians supported themselves through agriculture. Every year, reports from Greenwood listed more families who left tipi clusters for cabins

A Teton Sioux give-away and feast in the late 19th century. In this ceremony, held to honor an individual, food and other possessions were shared, helping the needy in the community.

up and down the valley. Every year, more land came into cultivation by Indian farmers.

Yanktons faced many obstacles as they scattered. Drought, grasshoppers, early frost, or blizzard conditions destroyed their crops and killed their livestock. Every few years, a great flood on the Missouri caused by springtime ice jams and melting snow washed away their cabins and farm buildings. For instance, in the spring of 1881 an ice jam at the narrow below Fort Randall backed up a lake that swamped the White Swan village of the upper bands. When the jam broke loose, a flood swept many Yankton log houses away from valley farms below Greenwood. Traditionalists from the upper bands, trying to prevent the destruction of tipi villages and the breakup of communal land, caused trouble for farmers of the lower bands.

Many tribal members left band villages, nevertheless, to try family farming. Having this experience, these people at least found it easy to understand and accept the General Allotment Act passed by Congress in 1887. According to this act, each Indian on nearly every western reservation was to receive an individual farm of about 160 acres. Federal officials would sell the surplus acreage within reservation boundaries for settlement by non-Indians. In passing this law, Congress hoped that the Indians would take up family farming or ranching on private land and give up their tribal affiliations. They would gain incentive for self-sufficiency through personal ownership, and learn farming techniques along with other things about non-Indian culture by contact with their new, non-Indian neighbors.

Upper-band leaders objected to these changes and led demonstrations, protesting loudly at the agency. They wrote letters of protest to Washington, D.C., as well. Despite this, the first allotment procedures were completed by 1894. Under strong pressure from federal officials, the tribe sold more than half its land to the United States by "congressional agreement" in 1896. Within a decade, non-Indians, mainly Czechs from eastern Europe with experience in agriculture, had settled on most of the surplus land. The new settlers founded the towns of Wagner and Lake Andes. Railroad builders laid track across the northern half of the reservation, where most white settlers were living. Personnel at Greenwood as-

An army tent next to round-log cabins on a Yankton reservation farm allotment. Sioux people lived in tents in the summer because the log cabins were confining and poorly ventilated.

sured officials in Washington, D.C., that the merger of Yanktons with mainstream society was only a matter of time.

On this reservation, there was confusion over allotment. Families that had prospered on assignments before 1887 refused to give up their cabins and improvements as agents assigned other names to their tracts of land. As a compromise, officials divided many allotments into two parcels of land: one consisting of a homestead in the valley, and the second of productive farmland without buildings up on the prairie. For a decade or more, families with divided allotments occupied two or three types of housing as they migrated back and forth according to their seasonal needs. They camped on their prairie farmland in tipis or U.S. Army tents from spring to fall to work their fields, but returned to their log homes in the valley for the cold winter months. Others replaced the valley homes with log houses on their prairie land as quickly as possible.

To improve housing conditions, as well as to reduce mobility, officials introduced two types of frame structures in the 1890s. One was a tiny cabin. A cluster of these went up at the southwest corner of Greenwood, which local residents called mile-square housing because it was situated on the section or square mile of land that contained the agency. These small houses were for elders and other people who could not care for themselves. By making special provision for them, younger men

and women would be released to concentrate on developing their farms. The retired occupants had shelter free of charge close to mission and agency personnel and under the protection of tribal police. The issue clerk and agency physician were close at hand. To an outsider this retirement facility may have looked a lot like the legendary slave-hut community of the Old South. But it provided shelter and protection to many aging Yanktons for more than 50 years.

The second type of structure was called the issued-house (or issue-house by tribal members) because it was issued to new allottees by the Bureau of Indian Affairs. This was an innovation of greater importance. It measured 18 by 24 feet and was divided into 2 rooms by a single partition containing a half chimney for one all-purpose stove. It had two windows and one door. There was no ventilating system, but as the issue-house sagged on its rock foundation, holes and cracks opened up, letting in northern breezes. Eventually, most issue-houses became so difficult to heat in winter that their occupants abandoned them or put them to use for storage. They were in demand for a time, however, because they were prefabricated, inexpensive, and easy to set up. Some housed families with as many as 16 members. None were issued at Greenwood after 1912, but with additions several issue-houses remained in service until the 1960s.

While some allottees moved into log cabins and issue-houses on their allot-

TRADITIONAL INDIAN TRAILS

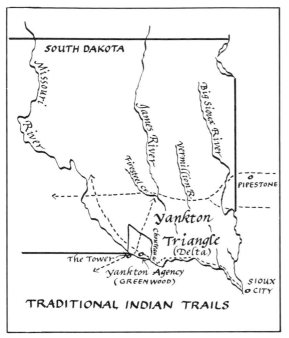

TRADITIONAL INDIAN TRAILS

Traditional trails of the Sioux crisscrossed the Triangle, or Delta, where Yanktons lived. When whites settled on the Triangle, Yanktons moved to the much smaller reservation.

ments, others used proceeds from crop or land sales to build homes on their own. These matched the best of those constructed by the Czech farmers and ranchers. When federal inspectors visited the Indian farms from 1912 to 1915, they photographed homes to show when they returned to Washington, D.C. Here and there a tipi was displayed on a farm site as a sign of traditionalism, but adaptation to non-Indian architecture was more evident. By then, living standards had improved

enough to convince officials that Yanktons were on the verge of being absorbed into the mainstream.

The decision to settle the Yanktons on scattered housing was a strategic ploy designed to isolate them from relatives and traditions. Families were separated, removed from village communities, and unable to participate in special events and religious ceremonies. Most of the time, Yanktons were bound to land and livestock. Only on weekends and holidays were they able to join relatives and friends for social affairs or religious activities.

Through the early reservation years no one provided greater inspiration in encouraging the Yanktons to take up new ways than Struck-by-the-Ree. According to legend, as an infant in 1804 he had been wrapped in the flag of the United States by the explorers Lewis and Clark, and honored with their prediction that he would grow up to be a man of peace. At about age 50, he began to fulfill the prophecy when he succeeded War Eagle to become head chief and principal speaker for the tribe. In those capacities, he was most persuasive in the decision by Yanktons to stand alone among Sioux tribes in refusing to take up arms against the United States. The head chief kept other leaders from organizing resistance to federal policies. He urged family heads to farm and went personally into the field with implements to do work long regarded as appropriate only for women and teenage children. He used his great skills of orating to prevent angry young men from joining leaders of upper bands in opposition to allotment. Chief Struck-by-the-Ree supported federal policies, yet he retained respect and obedience from most Yankton people until his death in 1888. He was the most important influence in this tribe's adjustment to non-Indian ways. While he lived and afterward, other band chiefs followed the lead of Old Strike in cultural change.

Others who had special significance were leading missionaries. Their goals were to teach basic skills in reading, writing, and arithmetic, and to entice Yanktons into accepting non-Indian ways—especially to replace the Sacred Pipe religion with Christianity. Father De Smet was the first to bring information about Christ to the Yankton Triangle when he visited in 1839. Catholic priests as well as lay leaders from Protestant missions stopped by from time to time. In the spring of 1869, Presbyterian minister John P. Williamson moved to Greenwood from Santee, Nebraska, with his wife and family to become the first resident ordained missionary to the Yankton people.

Doubtless Reverend Williamson had greater influence than any other missionary who served in Sioux Country because of his unusual upbringing. His had been the first recorded birth of a non-Indian in Minnesota outside of the military base at Fort Snelling. He had grown up at a remote mission station built by his father near the trading

John Williamson covered his original log church with siding and used it as his home and office after building the Presbyterian church next door.

post of trader Joseph Renville at Lac qui Parle. The nearest people, and his childhood friends, were Sioux. He grew up in a tribal environment, speaking Sioux language as well as English, and understanding Indian ways as well as those of his parents. Later, drawing on knowledge gained in childhood, Williamson wrote the first substantial dictionary in Sioux language. After coming to Greenwood, he founded the newspaper published at Santee in two languages, through which the Sioux and non-Indians learned about each other. He served as counselor, interpreter, and mediator for tribal members as they struggled with adjustment. He founded more than a dozen missions outside of the Yankton reservation, and also served for a short time as the U.S. agent for the Santees who settled near Flandreau.

When he came to Greenwood, he first lived with his family and ministered in a cabin made of hewn logs, which he cut upstream on an island and floated down to Greenwood on a raft. Within a year, he built a frame church next door, which survives as the Presbyterian facility of the longest uninterrupted service on any Sioux reservation. Then he covered the log cabin with siding and used it as an office and home for his family. To this center Williamson later added three satellite stations for Yanktons elsewhere on the reservation: the Hill Church, the Cedar Church, and the School in the Woods. The latter was abandoned in the 1880s, but Williamson Chapel at Greenwood,

Hill Church, and Cedar Church doubled as places of worship and day schools into the 20th century. In the mid-1920s, Yankton parishioners took over Williamson Chapel and dedicated a new brick church next door. Lay leaders have kept the three Presbyterian centers in operation as religious and cultural institutions down to the present day.

A few months after Williamson settled at Greenwood, Episcopal missionary Joseph Cook showed up. About three years later William Hobart Hare arrived. He was the first Episcopal bishop to Sioux people west of Minnesota and for a time made his headquarters at Greenwood. Neither Cook nor Hare ever grasped Indian culture the way Williamson did, but both adjusted quickly and built a system of chapels and schools to compete with those of the Presbyterians. They replaced a temporary log chapel with Holy Fellowship Church in Greenwood, which Bishop Hare used as a cathedral until he moved to Sioux Falls. Father Cook opened satellite chapels called Holy Name, St. Philip the Deacon, and Chapel of the Holy Comforter at Point of Timber. The latter washed away in the Great Flood of 1881, but the others remained in use. Today worship continues at Holy Fellowship, Holy Name, and St. Philip's churches, which stand in good repair under tribal lay leadership.

Williamson and Cook ran day schools at the chapels, and through them offered a variety of services. For

St. Paul's Boarding School for boys (left) and Emmanuel School for girls, built in the 1870s. The girls' school soon closed, and St. Paul's later became a federal government day school.

parishioners, they handled correspondence, arranged to enroll advanced students in religious schools off the reservation, and served as interpreters and moderators when officials from Washington, D.C., arrived on important business. Cook even provided health care, including minor surgery, at a clinic in Greenwood, apparently without training or license.

Bishop Hare specialized in setting up boarding schools. The first was St. Mary's Episcopal School for Girls, off the reservation at nearby Springfield. He then opened St. Paul's Boarding School for boys and Emmanuel House for girls, both at Greenwood. The bishop thought it necessary to isolate Indian youngsters from tribal culture so they could learn non-Indian ways without interference.

The Episcopalians and Presbyterians shared a dual mission, which they went about in somewhat different ways. Presbyterians believed that personal conversion to Christianity had to come first. Secular education would follow naturally, and adaptation to non-Indian society would be the inevitable result. Episcopalians believed that formal education should come first, and that Christianization would follow gradually within the mission environment. Neither group ever discussed the constitutional principles of separation of church and state, nor did federal officials until late in the 1890s. Missionaries used federal funds to support

The boarding school behind the two original churches founded by Father Sylvester. After he arrived in 1920, Yankton Catholics finally had churches and schools of their own.

formal education as they worked for mission societies in the East to convert Indian souls.

Williamson outlived Cook and Hare. By the time of his death in 1917, the Episcopal boarding schools at Greenwood had been closed for more than a decade. All central missions and satellite churches on the reservation had ceased to function as day schools. Management of chapels and grounds were being transferred to Indian lay leaders, who appeared to have rejected tribal religion for Christianity.

But this was not quite the reality. The religion practiced in reservation churches became a blend of Christian and Sioux beliefs. As a result, reserva-tion Christianity is not quite the same as non-Indian Christianity; it has evolved as an ecumenical blend de-signed to honor both traditions.

This blend of tribal beliefs and Christian dogma was as unacceptable to the early Protestant missionaries as it became to the first resident Catholic priest. Roman Catholic clergy had vis-ited occasionally since Father De Smet's brief appearance in 1839 to serve mass and offer instruction. After the reser-vation was founded, lay leaders looked after a small congregation headquar-tered in a home a few miles north of Greenwood (at the grounds of the pres-ent Marty Mission). The parishioners wanted a priest of their own. They talked to the bishop of Sioux Falls, traveled to St. Meinrad Abbey in Indiana, and offered land at a reasonable price. For a long time, their request was not filled, because there were so few Catholic missionaries to serve so many reservations in Sioux Country. Finally, in 1920, the Benedictine father Sylvester Eisenman accepted assignment to found Marty Mission, named for Martin Marty, the first Catholic bishop of South Dakota. By the time Father Sylvester died in 1948, he had established a major boarding school there. It remained under Catholic management until the Benedictines signed it over to the Yanktons in 1975 to be operated as a tribal school. Under the Benedictines, it served not only Yankton students, but also those from numerous other tribes who came by the bus- and truckload every fall. Father Sylvester completed St. Paul's Church to hold Yankton Catholics together. Known as the Queen of the Prairie, it stands majestically today to commemorate the work of Father Sylvester and as the central parish for Catholic congregations in Greenwood and Lake Andes. From the rectory next door, priests have gone out to minister to and look after the social or material needs of parishioners for more than half a century. Missionaries were selective in changing Yankton culture. They supported the use of tribal language in the belief that forced culture change and Christianization would be accomplished more efficiently if English were not forced immediately on the Indians. They encouraged a blend of Indian and non-Indian customs, so long as retained traditions did not hinder adjustment to non-Indian habits and beliefs. They approved of many Indian activities that did not challenge their efforts to turn Yanktons into productive citizens.

But missionaries of all three denominations stood sternly against anything that interfered with certain aspects of cultural adjustment. They supported federal officials in efforts to replace traditional tribal government headed by chiefs with an elected assembly of community representatives and a business committee. Missionaries worked as hard as the agents to suppress the giveaway and other sharing practices that they felt were undermining Indian adaptation to free enterprise. Most of all, they tried to eliminate every trace of the traditional Sacred Pipe religion, and demanded that it be totally replaced by Christian beliefs. Although missionaries did not succeed as well as they intended in changing spiritual life, they were equal partners with agency personnel in trying to bring Indians into mainstream society as citizens.

Federal officials gladly gave them subsidies to build and operate Episcopal and Presbyterian mission stations for educational use across the reservation. At the same time, agency personnel introduced their own educational efforts. Most important was the Government Boarding School at Greenwood, which opened in 1882 and ran for nearly 40 years. Like Bishop Hare's boarding institutions, it isolated chil-

THE YANKTON SIOUX RESERVATION

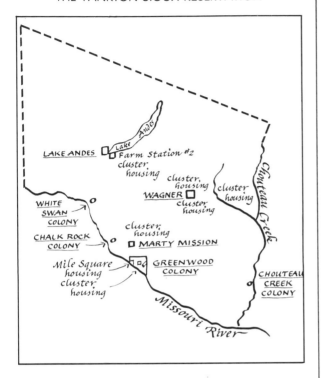

dren from tribal influence as it gave them the standard elementary school curriculum of the period for half of every school day. On a regular schedule, half of the students studied books in classrooms in the morning and received instruction in practical skills in the afternoon. The remaining half of the students learned practical tasks in the morning and went to their books in the afternoon. Every month the groups exchanged schedules. Girls learned the usual domestic arts of cooking, sewing, and housekeeping according to non-Indian standards. Boys worked on the farm of the Greenwood Government Boarding School, where they produced food as they learned to milk cows, care for livestock, raise grain, and produce truck-farm crops. The government school forbade students to use the Sioux language or to participate in Indian social and religious events during the academic year. The students were educated to adopt the ways of American citizens and to follow their parents into family farming and ranching.

Immediately after initial allotment proceedings ended in 1894, agency officials divided the reservation into two farm jurisdictions to hasten the adjustment of adults. District #1 centered at Greenwood. District #2 opened for the upper bands under an assistant farmer, who lived at a demonstration farm near the edge of Lake Andes until 1932. The farmer at Greenwood and his assistant at Lake Andes taught Yanktons techniques of using horse-drawn machinery, selective livestock breeding, dry farming on arid land, and maintaining agricultural equipment. The assistant farmer at Lake Andes also served as subagent to manage land affairs for tribal members, look after Indian bank accounts, arrange the education of children, supervise the tribal police in his district, and so on. In addition, he, like all other federal employees, promoted adaptation to outward symbols of non-Indian culture. Sometimes agency officials hired only those Indian men who had cut their hair short, and who wore clothing issued by the government.

Federal policy was to undermine all

An issue-house originally built in the 1890s north of Greenwood was improved with the additions to the right, and remained in use until the 1960s. The Bureau of Indian Affairs provided the two-room issue-houses so the Yanktons could live on their farm allotments.

institutions of cultural tradition. Only the Sun Dance was made illegal by formal order on the Yankton Reservation. Agency workers offered alternate activities and exerted social pressure to weaken traditional practices or drive them underground. Without even making most Indian customs illegal, officials worked steadily to undermine the religion of the Sacred Pipe, to eliminate traditional dancing, and to prevent give-aways. At special public ceremonies, traditionalists gave away personal possessions in public displays of sacrifice, or in honor of relatives or friends. To compete with such traditional activities, agency personnel established the Yankton Sioux Agricultural Fair Ground near Greenwood, where they sponsored Fourth-of-July celebrations and agricultural fairs every fall. At these events, some tribal members played Indian games, ate traditional food, and participated in horse races under agency supervision. They were also treated to non-Indian cuisine, such as fresh beef cooked and served with other foods. They received prizes for outstanding agricultural produce and were thus encouraged to become better farmers and ranchers. On the Yankton and other Sioux reservations, agricultural

(continued on page 52)

Sweatlodge used for fasting at Pipestone Quarry in 1972. It is covered with canvas, but is otherwise similar to the buffalo-robe-covered lodges used by Sioux at the same place three centuries earlier.

THE SACRED
PIPE RELIGION

The Sacred Pipe came to the Sioux long, long ago. Two scouts in search of food for their tribe during a period of famine encountered a beautiful woman. She gave them the original Pipe and taught them the ceremonial rites that govern its use. After leaving the Pipe in the care of tribal leaders, she turned into the White Buffalo Calf and moved silently away. Since that time, Sioux spiritual leaders have continued to use replicas of the original Pipe in the healing ritual known as *Inipi* and in other ceremonies held at the request of a member of the community.

The appearance of White Buffalo Calf Woman to the Sioux was no less magical than the virgin birth and the resurrection of Christ. It could in no way have been inspired by Christian teaching, because the Inipi liturgy was used for Father Louis Hennepin, one of the first Christian visitors, when he came to Sioux Country in the spring of 1680.

Like all Inipis, this ceremony was held in a sweatlodge, where Father Hennepin experienced a ritual sweatbath as a medicine man prayed for his recovery from illness. The sweatlodge was built of ash or willow saplings and covered by buffalo-skin robes. Today it is covered with canvas or blankets. The person who comes for prayer or healing sits on the ground inside the sweatlodge. Rocks heated in a fire are brought in, small amounts of water are poured over the red-hot stones at brief intervals, and heat and steam build up inside the lodge.

Just as there are numerous denominations and practices in Christianity, so are there many ways in which the Sioux call on the Sacred Pipe. At frequent intervals during an Inipi or other ceremony, the medicine man may cleanse the body of the person in need with stalks of sage, practice the laying-on of hands, and seek specific divine intervention. During a sweatlodge ceremony held for a man, a medicine woman who has had a special vision may guard the door and hold the Pipe. A medicine woman also conducts sweatlodge ceremonies for women who are in need. Medicine men and women alike may conduct the ceremonies only after they have fasted and have received spiritual guidance in a vision quest. Each leader is guided by fundamental beliefs and procedures handed down for generations, yet each may use unique procedures personally revealed in a vision quest.

Ceremonies are held when they are requested by an individual, not according to any calendar or schedule. They may take place in sweatlodges or homes, are always conducted in total darkness, and last from one to several hours. At each of these, people gather in a circle. The medicine man offers special prayers. He and his assistants sing a series of appropriate songs, usually 20 or more of them. The ceremony provides an opportunity for participants to call upon the spirits, offer prayers, receive responses from the spirits (which sometimes order specific types of penance), and conduct special procedures to usher the spirits out with thanks. After each ceremony there is a feast. This is a time of social fellowship, an occasion for leaders to give orations on topics of community interest and teach cultural traditions.

Central to this religion is fasting, a form of personal sacrifice used to achieve spiritual renewal or receive a personal revelation in a vision quest. The Sioux have believed that the Great Spirit, the Supreme Being, may appear to them with a personal message in a vision, and they have known from experience that such visions might come only to those who have made special preparations and fasted as a sign of devotion, if spiritual forces chose to appear. Even without receiving a vision, though, the person who fasted has gained intellectual renewal and spiritual commitment. Yet no one could achieve leadership as a medicine man or medicine woman without having had a personal vision.

Seven fasting procedures are available. Most frequently used over the last century have been quiet meditation at an isolated hilltop or in a sweatlodge. The most revered and rigorous fasting procedure is participation in the Sun Dance. Whatever procedure is used, the person may choose whether to fast for one, two, three, or four days and nights.

A person who intends to fast prepares a pipe filled with tobacco and brings it to a medicine man. The medicine man smokes the pipe in ritual fashion as a signal that fasting may take place. The medicine man (or medicine woman, if the fasting person is female) attends the person throughout the fast. So do fellow believers and the spiritual manifestations of winged and four-legged creatures.

Sun Dance participants might, in an extreme act of personal sacrifice, pierce their skin with a sharp instrument and tie on thin strips of rawhide. Non-Indians were shocked by this in the 19th century, and as a result the ceremony was prohibited by federal order in the 1880s. However, the Sun Dance did not come to a halt. It was carried on surreptitiously for some 80 years and finally came into the open again during the 1960s.

Preparing to participate in the Sun Dance takes several months. It involves physical conditioning and intellectual meditation as well as spiritual cleansing through Inipi ceremonies. At the Sun Dance itself, many people gather to fast and dance together. Skin piercing is optional and is considered

A fire pit has been dug next to the framework for a sweatlodge at Pipestone Quarry. Stones heated in the fire will be put in the lodge, creating steam when water is poured over them.

to be only one part of personal sacrifice in search of spiritual guidance. Many dancers who fast do not pierce. Most agonizing is the period of up to four days without food or water in hot weather.

People fast mainly in early summer, near the time "when the choke cherries turn black" as they ripen. An experience of fasting serves not only those who make the sacrifice, but also the entire congregation. Like a Christian revival meeting, fasting renews personal commitment and sustains the group throughout the year. It also gives all in attendance the opportunity to ask for group prayers in support of a request for healing or other needs.

Like other Sioux today, most Yankton people who continue to practice traditional worship see merit in all forms of prayer. They view the way of the Sacred Pipe as an equivalent to Christianity. An ecumenical people, they have been receptive to Christianity while they have been generous in accepting in their midst outsiders who wish to share in traditional Indian religious ways. ▲

(continued from page 47)

fairs operated under Indian management but at agency expense with agency supervision from the 1890s to the 1930s.

As a substitute for the get-togethers for worship with the Sacred Pipe, agents encouraged attendance at annual convocations held by all three Christian denominations each summer or fall on various reservations. Agents even approved and encouraged the use of seven dance halls, run by dance-hall chiefs who represented seven communities across the reservation, to bring dancing under agency supervision. Yanktons could assemble at these only on weekends, usually with supervisors present to prevent give-aways and other traditional activities. Unofficially, federal employees at Greenwood let it be known that only people of middle age or older could dance. Young adults could come to watch, and children should not even get close enough to see adults dancing. This way, they hoped, the traditional powwow could be phased out in 20 or 30 years.

By many means, Yanktons were more enticed than forced to adopt non-Indian customs. Within half a century, most officials thought Yanktons were ready to move from tribalism to citizenship, and they began to cut back on their training efforts. In 1902 they stopped providing free supplies to those in need across the reservation, and in 1908 they paid the last annuities due under the 1858 treaty.

In 1903 the superintendent, as the head of the agency was now called, de-

Ration issue day on the Pine Ridge reservation in the early 1880s. When non-Indian hunters nearly exterminated the buffalo, the Sioux and other Plains tribes had no meat. Agencies gave out rations of beef and other food items as annuities owed to tribal members under treaties.

Agency officials sponsored agricultural fairs to encourage Indians to become farmers. This float was displayed at Fort Yates on the Standing Rock reservation.

clared that tribal government by chiefs was a thing of the past. Earlier, traditional chiefs who died had been replaced with men "made chief" by agents as a reward for their willingness to support federal policies. In 1891 these "BIA chiefs" had cooperated with agency personnel to set up a Speaking Council of 100 elected community representatives. Almost immediately this single-house legislature delegated its power over critical matters to a business committee and accepted the superintendent as its chairman. With that advantage, the superintendent was able to declare that chiefs were no longer recognized by federal authorities on the reservation, even though the last chief did not die until 1920. The business committee disappeared for lack of use by 1912. Yanktons no longer needed a government of their own, thought federal officials, because they were nearly ready to abandon tribalism. All that remained was to formally transfer control over allotments to their Indian owners, and to release the funds remaining in Indian accounts from the previous sale or lease of communal real estate and allotments. The Yanktons would soon be full citizens and self-sufficient farmers like other Americans. ▲

Black Eagle, also known as John Ree, was the nephew of Struck-by-the-Ree. He served as a scout under General Alfred Sully to maintain peace between Indians and non-Indians in the 1860s, and later became an important band chief.

YANKTONS FALL
ON
HARD TIMES

By the early 1920s, most Yanktons had been given control over their allotments and money from the sale or lease of their land. The General Allotment Act of 1887 had provided that patents (certificates of ownership) to Indian allotments be held in trust by federal authorities for 25 years. This waiting period was intended to prevent the recipients from selling the land and spending the proceeds foolishly before they had learned the value of private ownership. Subsequently the rules were changed to speed up the process. The "trust period" was reduced so the Indians could own their allotment outright as soon as they were declared "competent" by the secretary of the interior to manage private land. By 1920 the vast majority of Yanktons, like non-Indians, held *patents-in-fee* to their own land. Now they could lease or sell part or all of their allotments by personal choice. With the fee patent went citizenship. (For those who still held trust patents, Congress granted citizenship in 1924.)

By that time, almost all monies left in the general account of the tribe had been distributed in equal shares to tribal members. Most Yanktons gained control of their Individual Indian Money Accounts at local banks. After 1916 scores of allotments were listed for sale in every issue of the newspaper *Lake Andes Wave*. Children went off to boarding schools. A few Yanktons moved to Michigan for work in the growing automobile industry. Some traveled in Wild West shows. Many took seasonal jobs with harvest crews. Reservation population declined, and external signs of Indianness seemed to be growing faint.

Officials in Washington, D.C., regarded these changes as signs that acculturation was successful, but their optimism was not justified by conditions on the reservation. U.S. inspectors who came to evaluate tribal progress between 1912 and 1915 described only those Yanktons who were most successful at farming and ranching, and who blended into non-Indian

LAND CLAIMED BY YANKTON TRIBE,
1770–1858, WITH DATES OF CESSION
TO THE UNITED STATES

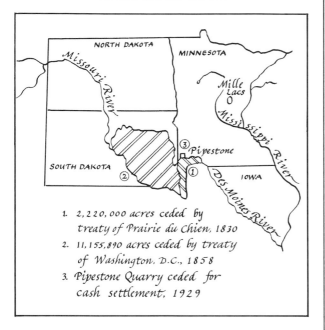

1. 2,220,000 acres ceded by treaty of Prairie du Chien, 1830
2. 11,155,890 acres ceded by treaty of Washington, D.C., 1858
3. Pipestone Quarry ceded for cash settlement, 1929

society with ease. The inspectors praised their accomplishment of having crop and livestock production as great as that of their non-Indian neighbors, but made no mention of those Yanktons who had little success on the land. They featured in their reports those tribal members who dressed like non-Indians, spoke English as a first or second language, and sent their children to integrated schools. These reports failed to mention Yanktons who clung to traditional ways and continued to enroll their children in boarding schools. With support from statistics, every year the inspectors could boast about increasing numbers of children who were tested and found to be free from tuberculosis and certain other communicable diseases and then enrolled at integrated district schools. Christian congregations continued to grow as lay leaders took charge of reservation parish activities. Traditional ceremonies and giveaways grew scarce. The superintendent at Greenwood reinforced the impression created by the inspectors' reports that there was a decline in tribal attachments of almost every kind.

Similar optimistic reports were coming from other reservations across the West. To determine the extent of real change, and to gather information to use in the next phase of acculturation, the commissioner of Indian affairs ordered a survey in 1922 of every Indian family on every allotment on nearly every reservation in the West. American taxpayers had spent hundreds of millions of dollars to hasten change in the Indian cultures. Tribal groups had used up their annuities and land sale proceeds in efforts to gain self-sufficiency. It was time to see how effective agency personnel and missionaries had been. With this information in hand, a five-year plan for further advancement would be drafted for each tribe.

Officials at Greenwood gathered data and sent in detailed reports. Their "Industrial Survey" of Indian farmstead productivity must have shocked officials in Washington, D.C. In a tribe with more than 2,000 members, only 3 or 4 family heads supported their families by farming and ranching. There was a shortage of food and other necessities. There was widespread discouragement. Many people were drinking alcoholic beverages. Numerous houses were in disrepair.

The survey made it clear that most Yanktons had fallen on hard times. One cause was a regional decline in prices for agricultural output in the early 1920s. Hundreds of non-Indian farmers and ranchers were driven from their land in bankruptcy. Another was false optimism created by earlier reports—a sense that Yankton people were at the verge of being able to cope on their own. Intent on earning the approval of superiors for their success, federal employees at every level had failed to report that only a small number of tribal members were able to get along without assistance. Greenwood Agency officials had brushed aside warnings by realistic employees about the consequences of awarding title to land without considering individual circumstances. From 1916 to 1920, more Yankton land was offered for sale than non-Indians could buy, because the Indians needed money to purchase necessities. Critics were correct in accusing some Yanktons of spending their money on race horses, automobiles, and other nonessentials. But far more people used up the personal resources gained through the sales of allotments in order to survive. By 1922 much of the Yanktons' land and nearly all of their money was gone.

Then came a time of nationwide economic disaster. In part it was brought

Sioux men clearing land for road construction on the Standing Rock reservation in the 1930s, a project of the Civilian Conservation Corps-Indian Division (CCC-ID).

Telephone lines were installed on the Standing Rock reservation in the 1930s, through a program of the CCC-ID.

about by the drought and searing heat that turned the Great Plains region into a dust bowl during the early 1930s. Crops failed. Livestock sickened and died. People lost their land, their livelihoods, their homes. In 1933 Greenwood became a subagency of the Rosebud Agency about 150 miles away. Now Yanktons received even less consideration than before because the superintendent was giving preferential

treatment to people on the Rosebud Reservation where he was based. At this low point in their history, the Yankton came close to starvation. Father Sylvester opened a soup kitchen at Marty Mission to keep his parishioners alive. The subagent at Greenwood warned of general disaster unless federal help came soon.

Conditions in the Great Depression years were like this for everyone across the West, not only for Indians. After his inauguration in 1933, President Franklin Roosevelt promised a New Deal for all Americans in need. The new commissioner of Indian affairs, John Collier, provided a special Indian New Deal for reservation residents. Yanktons became eligible for assistance through New Deal programs for all citizens, as well as from the Indian New Deal for residents of a reservation.

Within a year, direct relief came with the distribution of livestock purchased by the Emergency Relief Administration (ERA). Federal agents bought cattle to subsidize ranchers who were not otherwise able to sell their animals and offered them for slaughter to people in need of food. On Indian reservations, these cattle were marked with the brand ERA, to distinguish them from Indian Department (ID) cattle intended as the breeding stock to enlarge the herds of tribal members. With tongue in cheek, Indian people interpreted the ERA brand to mean "eat 'em right away." They did so as fast as the livestock arrived.

Tribal members also received direct

relief in the form of packaged surplus food, purchased by the U.S. Department of Agriculture to take excess farm products off the market and provide income for producers. Included were portions of sugar, flour, cheese, canned meat, cereal, and other staple items. For nearly 10 years, food packages came directly from the federal Department of Agriculture. After New Deal programs shut down in 1942, surplus food distribution was integrated into state welfare systems. This program saved countless tribal members from starvation through the 1930s. Since then, department surplus commodities have been available to needy Indians and non-Indians alike through tribal committees or county welfare systems.

Along with direct relief came self-help opportunities of several kinds. Through the Works Progress Administration (WPA), Civilian Conservation Corps (CCC), and other programs of assistance to non-Indians, federal officials sought to improve the material economy of all citizens. In addition, they invited able-bodied Indians to work on special projects to improve life for themselves and their families. Men skilled in road or bridge construction and maintenance through previous employment on reservation roads were paid day-labor wages from an enlarged budget of the roads division in the Bureau of Indian Affairs. A family head who qualified could work only half-time, so that the available funds would stretch to help as many as possible. For hand labor, a person could earn up to $1.50 a day. A man who brought a team of horses could make $2.50 a day. As on all Sioux reservations, roads division employment was among the most important forms of self-help relief. It not only prevented hunger, but also improved reservation roads, making them fit for travel by bus, truck, and automobile for the first time.

Meanwhile the Civilian Conservation Corps, a federal program, had been launched. Its purpose was to provide employment for men across the country, while preserving natural resources. The workers received training, room and board, and a salary of $25 to $45 per month. Some Yanktons joined non-Indians at camps in Chamberlain and places nearby. In conjunction with the integrated CCC, a program labeled CCC-ID became available. The segregated CCC-ID brought young Indian men into tent camps to live and work full-time for lodging, board, and federal wages. Every enrollee had to send part of the pay to his family as he labored on projects related to conservation. There were no camps for Yanktons close to home, but one was created for them on the Rosebud Reservation. Here they built roads for fire protection, terraced hillsides to prevent erosion, built dams and spillways to hold floods under control, planted trees, poisoned destructive pests, and put up telephone systems to assure communication for fire control.

Another self-help program offered materials to any person who was skilled in their use to repair or improve houses

Song Hawk Dam was built on the Yankton reservation as a combined project of the CCC and the Works Progress Administration to prevent erosion, hold water for livestock, and provide for recreation.

and other buildings at allotment locations. Many people ordered shingles, siding, lumber, doors, windows, and internal trimming. Homes that had deteriorated without attention for many years were now restored to near original condition.

Some Yanktons were also employed on special projects on their own reservation through integrated CCC and WPA programs. They terraced pasture land on the Missouri Hills and constructed dams designed to prevent erosion, pool water for livestock, and provide recreation. The largest was Song Hawk Dam, at the east end of the reservation, which has continued to serve all three purposes down to the present. Other Yanktons found construction jobs through the WPA in building the new Indian hospital at Wagner.

Families in direst need went to live in John Collier's celebrated colonies. The commissioner felt that Indians would have a better life if they returned to their traditional communalism. He established more than a dozen colonies in Sioux Country with that in mind. Four of them were on the Yankton Reservation. The Indian office purchased land of marginal value for agriculture with authority from the Indian Reorganization Act of 1934, which provided for the eventual transfer of ownership to the tribe. The Indian Relief and Rehabilitation program paid most of the cost for development. At the largest colony, WPA money paid Indian workers to quarry chalk rock from a cliff on the nearby Missouri Hills and cut it into building blocks with a power saw. This project was known variously as Chalk Rock Rehabilitation Colony; Rising Hail Colony, after a local chief; Seven Mile Creek Colony, because it was constructed on a creek seven miles up the Missouri from Greenwood; and simply the Colony, for its prominence. It contained eight chalk-rock cabins and two old frame houses that had been on the land all along. Smaller colonies at Greenwood, White Swan, and Chouteau Creek had one, two, and four housing units, respectively.

Management authority for the 17 units and other facilities belonged to a special board of tribal members appointed by the superintendent. The board chose families in greatest need who were willing to turn over any personal possessions that might be of value to the enterprise when they entered the Colony. From the proceeds of their collective efforts they received shares of produce according to their labor and needs as long as they were there.

Officials bragged a great deal about the promise of these facilities. Housing units were rent free. Behind each home, a fence contained a chicken coop in which fowl were raised for food and eggs. Every colony had a large community garden, which members worked together. There was a canning kitchen to which tribal members on allotments as well as residents of the Colony could bring fruits and vegetables for preservation in metal cans, free of charge. At Chalk Rock Colony, there was a substantial dairy and horse barn and a large field set up for irrigated agriculture in the production of sorghum, wheat, oats, barley, corn, and hay. Most of this was fodder for livestock; little grain was sold.

The colonies represented only one of several efforts made by Indian New Deal administrators to encourage the recovery of tribal ways. Also important were projects to revive Indian arts and culture. On the Yankton Reservation, an important star-quilt industry was begun with a federal subsidy, and bead work was revived. Tribal members could again speak their own language without fear of punishment. Anyone, regardless of age, could go to dances at any time and attend traditional Pipe ceremonies. Even a new group that followed the Peyote religion, which had appeared near Greenwood about 1910, was no longer harassed so much by officials who mistook its members' ritual use of peyote for a drug cult.

Under Indian New Deal policies, traditional practices came into the open for the first time in two generations. To the surprise of no one on this reservation, Yanktons were ready. They had not lost the old ways, but only taken them underground for protection. ▲

Pretty Rock, or Felix Brunot, born in 1852, succeeded his father as a band chief when he was only 13 years old. This photo was taken before the young chief became the first Yankton to attend college. Without giving up traditions, he advocated cooperation and acculturation. He died in 1920, the last of the Yankton band chiefs.

TOWARD
TERMINATION
AND
ACCOMMODATION

About the only tradition that seemed beyond recovery was the communal life-style. After living for two generations in scatter housing under pressure to accept free enterprise and private ownership, Yanktons were no longer accustomed to sharing in this degree. At the colonies, they quarreled over the quantities of produce they received for their respective contributions. They blamed each other for capital losses when the barn at Seven Mile Creek burned from spontaneous combustion in the hay mow, for example, and when some cattle died of disease. Disillusioned by communal life, colony residents were eager to follow other tribal members in taking off-reservation employment when the opportunity arose during World War II. Few families lived in the communal environment of the colonies for more than a year, and only one or two for more than two years. Eventually, the United States turned the land and facilities over to the tribe. By 1950 there was only one family left

in a cabin at Seven Mile Creek to lease the land for cash. Twenty years later, only a ruin at Chalk Rock Colony and two cabins used at Chouteau Creek survived as reminders of a well-intentioned but unrealistic attempt by officials in the East to decide how Yankton people ought to live. In the late 1940s, those who had remained on the reservation returned to the scatter housing on their allotments, which they had improved somewhat with materials provided by the Indian New Deal. Few if any new houses were built on this reservation from the 1920s to the 1960s.

Yanktons also rejected a federal plan to revive tribal government, according to the terms of the Indian Reorganization (Wheeler-Howard) Act of 1934. Under this act, tribal adults were invited to vote on three things: (1) the idea of political revival under federal supervision, (2) a constitution and bylaws to become tribal law, and (3) the incorporation of a tribe into a body legally eligible to receive all federal benefits

Only a few abandoned buildings remain from Chalk Rock Colony, one of the short-lived communal farming settlements that Indian commissioner John Collier hoped would thrive.

due to tribes that would accept the terms of the act.

Among Sioux in the United States, only three reservation groups declined to set up Wheeler-Howard governments within a few years: those at Upper Agency of Minnesota, Standing Rock on the border between North and South Dakota, and the Yankton Reservation. Yanktons had approved their own constitution in 1932 at an assembly held at Lake Andes. By refusing to change it into a Wheeler-Howard government, they lost benefits and even federal recognition of their elected officials. Not until they approved constitutional revisions to the liking of federal officials in 1963 did they regain appropriate political recognition. Six years later, the Yanktons were detached from the Rosebud Agency and recovered full agency status at headquarters in Wagner. Even then, as a non-Wheeler-Howard tribe, Yankton people continued to be ineligible for many benefits provided only to those groups that had accepted federal supervision in tribal government during the 1930s, as Collier had urged them to do.

From about 1942 to the mid-1960s, slights by federal officials mattered little to most Yanktons because conditions in some ways improved for Indians across the country. After coming through the 1930s with help from Indian New Deal programs, Yanktons participated patriotically in efforts to win World War II. Many enlisted in the armed forces, and some saw combat overseas. Others held war-related jobs, from construction at the army air corps base near Rapid City, South Dakota, to employment at the Hanford Works, an atomic bomb development plant in the state of Washington. Still more Yanktons entered the agricultural work force of the region, which was shorthanded at a time when there was great demand for farm products.

The decline of the Indian population on the reservation, which began during the war years, continued into the 1950s. Now federal administrators joined Congress to abandon all efforts to restore Indianness. After Commissioner Collier retired, officials returned to the integration policy they had been pursuing from the middle of the 19th century through the 1920s. In 1946 Congress created the Indian Claims Commission to pay awards to tribes as final compensation for wrongs done them. Mainly, the commission recommended compensation by Congress for "unconscionable consideration" (inadequate payment) for land sold by the tribe to the United States, or the mismanagement of tribal properties and affairs by agency or other federal employees in the past. At the same time, federal leaders either searched for means to dissolve tribes or abandoned them as recognized groups for which the United States retained any responsibility. This new policy was known as *termination*.

The termination movement took several forms. One was to substitute state programs and supervision of

In the 1930s, this Teton family had only an army tent in which to live.

tribes for federal supports and jurisdictional guarantees. Another was to give up federal responsibility for agency facilities. On the Yankton Reservation, numerous government facilities were abandoned or offered for sale, and Greenwood went into decline as a center of activity. Still another form of termination was the transfer or withdrawal of social services that had previously been provided by the Indian bureau. The Indian hospital at Wagner now became a public health service facility. Farm Station #2 at Lake Andes, the colony facilities, and some buildings in Greenwood were turned over to the tribe. A day school at Greenwood closed down.

The most dramatic change of all,

though, was the move to terminate federal responsibility for tribes through relocation. By means of the Voluntary Relocation Program of the 1950s and an Employment Assistance Program of the 1960s, special officers of the Indian bureau enticed Indians to leave reservations for industrial centers with token payments and glowing descriptions of job opportunities. Thus, lured by the relocation officer at Rosebud, Yanktons became prominent among Sioux fleeing reservations. Large numbers moved to towns and cities within the region, seeking education or jobs. Fewer moved as far away as Chicago, Denver, Dallas, Los Angeles, Seattle, St. Paul, and other industrial centers, where they accepted integration and long-term employment.

By the 1950s, only about 42,000 acres of Yankton Reservation land were still held as individual allotments or tribal acreage. This was less than 10 percent of the area that had been occupied by the tribe in 1859. The reservation population was now little more than 1,000. Federal officials contracted with historians and anthropologists to determine how many could exist decently depending on reservation resources without further assistance from the government, and to plan the relocation of the excess population. Reports on Yanktons were similar to those for other Sioux tribes. Relocation off the reservation should be encouraged. Those who remained would not survive from the land alone. Uncomplicated, clean, light industries seemed to hold the greatest promise for employing reservation residents productively.

Early in the 1960s, federal subsidies became available to build light industries on reservations across Sioux Country. More than 70 were attempted; fewer than a half-dozen survived. One reason was that many of the corporations that opened industries on Sioux reservations were mismanaged organizations that had sought federal aid in order to avoid bankruptcy. Another was that there had been too little investigation into the kinds of work that tribal groups might want to do. Worst of all, industrial managers showed little sensitivity to the culture of the Indian workers.

Because participation in cultural life is so compelling to traditional Indians, they suffer an unusual form of persecution for their occasional failure to appear on time at the workplace. Those who live on the reservation full-time travel to other reservations or to towns and cities on request. Urban Indian people go to the reservation when they are called. Traditional Yanktons travel frequently to share in weekend activities and special events. More often than not, the failure of a tribal member to show up on time for work five days a week is the result of such commitments. "Indian time" represents unavoidable obligation more often than personal preference. Traditionalists who lived on Indian time because they were involved with cultural activities were often fired.

Yanktons made two attempts to participate in this reservation-based indus-

Father William Fahsing teaches a Yankton to assemble electronic components for radios in the 1960s. The Greenwood Electronics Industry, built on the grounds of the Episcopal Holy Fellowship Church, was successful for a time, but ultimately failed because its management was unable to adapt to the perspective of the Indian workers.

trial movement. The first was initiated at Greenwood by a well-intentioned Episcopal priest, William Fahsing. Financed by the bishop of Sioux Falls, he set up Greenwood Electronics Industry to assemble components for radios and other electronic equipment in the 1960s, managing it himself with skills he had learned before entering the ministry. The plant did well for a time. Fahsing arranged work schedules according to Indian time; employees could work for a given number of hours each week or month without a commitment to be at the plant for a particular number of hours in any day. He offered a work environment that resembled a factory only in its possessing an assembly line. Unfortunately, Fahsing failed to ask if this was the kind of work that Yankton people wanted to do, and he openly criticized those who did not respond as he expected.

Many worked faithfully until the Episcopal diocese decided that light industry was not part of its calling and withdrew its support. Fahsing's superiors forced him to sell the plant to a corporation with headquarters in the city of Yankton. Quickly, the company's business managers imposed the industrial standards of non-Indian factories to improve efficiency and increase production. Indians who failed to show up for work eight hours every day on jobs assigned to them were fired. The industry collapsed in cultural misunderstanding.

A similar fate was in store for the tribal pork plant that opened at Wagner early in the 1970s. Tribal leaders contracted with Texas meat packers to build a meat processing and packing plant. The Texas experts would manage the plant for 10 years in partnership with the Yanktons, by which time they would receive a fair return on their investment. After a decade, they would withdraw, and control and ownership of the plant would belong exclusively to the tribe. With a contract to package meat for military use, the plant began operations in the hope of hiring several dozen Indians. Before long, however, rigid industrial rules and firings for Indian-time attendance reduced the tribal work force to a few and swelled the non-Indian work force to more than 30.

No Yanktons rose to the managerial positions which would have provided essential training for the time when the tribe would take over. Encouraged by militant Indian leaders in this region, young people moved in with light arms to occupy the plant. State officials showed up with troops. Local ranchers bearing deer rifles circled the plant in pickup trucks. High-ranking clergy and politicians intervened to prevent bloodshed. The Texans went home. The plant never opened again, despite several efforts by tribal leaders to make it the site of some light industry.

Benefits promised through the Great Society social and economic programs initiated by President Lyndon Johnson in the 1960s all but passed Yanktons by. They received very little

Modern homes were built at the old Farm Station #2 near Lake Andes in the 1970s. Because the buildings were near each other, or clustered, this is referred to as cluster housing.

assistance from programs of the Office of Economic Opportunity, for example, which came generously to other reservations for several years. Only a few new job opportunities were created on their reservation by federal programs. Aside from recovering full agency status in 1969, the only benefit they received was federal aid for new housing. In this, they shared with other tribes the most lasting benefit of Great Society years.

This help reached them belatedly in 1969 with the construction of both scatter and cluster housing. Quite a few Yanktons applied for new homes at isolated places on allotments still owned by their families or on communal tribal land, which they secured under long-term leases. Most of the homes looked like working-class suburban development dwellings, but they were painted in bright colors, doubtless because the paint they received came from surplus in federal inventories. Despite their gaudy appearance, which seemed out of place in Indian society, the houses were welcomed as the first new construction in some 50 years.

Those who preferred to live in cluster housing received small units at Greenwood, Marty, Wagner, and the old Farm District #2 station at Lake Andes. Two- or three-bedroom units formed developments in communities already equipped with utilities and urban services. Unfortunately, these locations had almost no recreational facilities and few jobs in reach. People of little means struggled to pay modest fees to occupy them. There is little squa-

lor in these areas, but there has been poverty bordering on hunger much of the time. There has been some crime, and as a result many elders fear to live in the cluster housing.

More housing came in the late 1970s and early 1980s. Tribal housing officials put up more scatter housing of split-level design on allotments or leased tribal land. They built three additional clusters east of Marty, north of Wagner, and in a rural setting at the northeast edge of the reservation.

With modern housing came the first new retirement facilities for elders since the mile-square housing was built at Greenwood in the 1890s. At Marty, Wagner, and Lake Andes, retirement homes were opened near cluster housing, where relatives, friends, and officials were available nearby.

The value of modern housing cannot be denied. Yet to visitors the appearance of the new structures only reinforces the impression of barrenness in reservation existence. With rare exceptions, Yankton home sites contain few trees, flower beds, or lawns, and what greenery there is has grown more by accident than design. Visitors are misled into believing that there is no more to reservation life than what they observe. From appearances, all too many have concluded that the reservation has become a place of abject poverty, wretched living conditions, and cultural waste. It is logical for them to pose this question: Should not the reservation at last be abandoned, as an act of humanity?

Non-Indians also question the value

Several housing units for Yankton elders were constructed near cluster housing at Lake Andes in the 1970s.

of reservations because they erroneously believe that tribal members use them as a refuge to escape from paying taxes and to thrive on "government checks" and other "payments." This myth is especially popular with non-Indians in such towns as Wagner and Lake Andes, where Indian people have cashed their checks and spent their money for 75 years or more.

Meanwhile, Yanktons have paid nearly all of the same kinds of taxes imposed on their non-Indian neighbors. They have paid income, sales, and excise taxes, as well as real estate assessments on allotments owned under fee patent. Their only exemption has been from levies on tribal-owned acreage and allotments still under federal trust patent.

Since the early 1900s, reservation residents have received few welfare benefits beyond those given to non-Indians in similar need. Most "government checks" contain lease monies paid through agency offices for allotments rented under contract by non-Indian farmers and ranchers. Additional "payments" have been individual shares of tribal funds created by land sales or congressional awards for unfair treatment in the past. On several occasions, Congress has compensated Yanktons for acreage sold to federal officials at prices below market values at the time, or for the careless if not dishonest management of their resources by agency employees. It is important to note that "offsets" (deductions) were subtracted from all claims awards paid to this tribe.

These subtractions were to offset, or compensate the government for, anything Yankton people received free-of-charge from federal agencies since the fur trade era. All checks and payments have been for the lease of lands or compensation for losses suffered by the tribe; Yankton people have received no gifts from American taxpayers!

Gossip among non-Indians about Indian checks and payments continues to damage race relations. The uninformed look down on tribal members as lazy welfare dependents. Yanktons deeply resent these false accusations as they struggle with a reservation unemployment rate in excess of 80 percent. Some tribal members regard this demeaning attack as yet another ruse to take what remains of tribal land.

So little is left. Most of it is grassland. Few acreages are managed or worked by tribal members for livelihood. What little remains would be vulnerable to loss were it not for a federal policy that gives tribal officials or Indian individuals the first chance to buy any Indian land that comes up for sale. This has allowed Yanktons to repurchase hundreds if not thousands of acres of their own land.

Little more than 42,000 acres of Indian land within the reservation boundaries is all that remains of the approximately 13.5 million acres in tribal possession at the time non-Indians first arrived. When asked why so many of them remain attached to such few acres with such little economic potential, Yanktons give three explanations. For one thing, the reservation is home. Understandably, Yanktons feel greater attachment to the rough lands they retain than do non-Indians to productive land on farms held by their families for less than a century.

A second reason is the value of the reservation as a retreat from the tension felt by those who are exposed daily to pressures from non-Indian society. "I feel relaxed. I can just take it easy amongst my own people," said the late Joseph Rockboy, who left the Greenwood area in 1922 to support a family off the reservation for more than 50 years. "I feel free when I cross Chouteau Creek and get on the reservation," says Leonard Bruguier, who as a youngster left a home below Greenwood for opportunity through education at Yankton city.

More important is the third explanation. The reservation preserves Indian culture, which survives best in isolation from daily ridicule by non-Indians. After living for two centuries at the front line of contact, tribal members are effective in using scattered acreages to protect the beliefs and practices that make them distinctively Indian. ▲

Feather In His Ear, who led the upper bands in opposing allotment and organized religion, is remembered as the band chief who sacrificed most to preserve tradition in the first decades of reservation life. His name is a mistranslation of his Sioux name, Wiyaka Napin, which really means Feather Necklace.

SURVIVAL
OF
YANKTON CULTURE

The most important traditions that the Yanktons preserve are their language and religion. It is these that attach them to the reservation despite all efforts that have been made over time to remove them from it.

Many Yanktons speak a dialect of the Sioux language on the streets of Wagner and Lake Andes as well as in their reservation homes. Its use provides a shield of privacy, creates an atmosphere of Indianness, and preserves points of view and philosophies that set Yankton culture apart from mainstream American society. Sioux language expresses complicated concepts in single words and phrases that defy translation because no equivalent ideas exist in Anglo-American society.

Many words hold hidden meanings to traditionalists that few non-Indians ever come to understand. For example, a simple definition of *mitakuyase* is all of my relatives, and of *oyate*, nation. But when the two words are used together in the context of religion, they contain rich philosophical connotations. The term *mitakuyase* refers to all things around a person, past and present. Included are not only humans of immediate and extended families, but also winged creatures, for instance, and four-legged beings. Thus *mitakuyase oyate* refers to nation groups with spiritual as well as physical qualities. When called upon for help, they respond as fellow members of creation in support of humans with needs. Highest among winged creatures are Eagles. Special among four-legged nation groups are Bears and Elks, among others. A traditionalist, in the course of a ceremony, may say "mitakuyase" and call upon the *wanbli oyate*, nation of Eagles, or the *hekhaka oyate*, nation of Elk. By using these words, the speaker calls to the minds of listeners aspects of philosophy completely foreign to outsiders and wholly essential to traditional Indian ways. When used in a social context, however, the term *hekhaka* creates an image of love and virility. A ceremony

A Lawanpi, *or song service, altar. Earth and eagle feathers are surrounded by (clockwise from top left) jars with cloth flags, in colors that represent spirits to be invoked at the ceremony; a canister of water; a peace pipe; and cedar, used to purify the altar and people at the service.*

that appeals to the Elk (which is evidenced by the use of the color yellow) is used in courtship to express admiration for a member of the opposite sex. For these and hundreds of other Sioux terms, no English synonyms suffice to communicate the multiple layers of tribal tradition.

Another vehicle of cultural tradition preserved by reservation boundaries is Indian religion. The Sacred Pipe way differs little today from the description written by Father Louis Hennepin in 1680 after medicine men held a series of sweatlodge *Inipi* ceremonies to cure his ailments. Missionaries and federal employees at Greenwood have used almost every means except law to destroy the Pipe, but Yankton traditionalists preserved it underground. Since the 1930s, the ways of the Pipe have surfaced in a renaissance that allows change in procedure without loss of meaning. Several Yanktons have stood out as leaders of major ceremonies, and they continue to participate actively in the Sun Dance as well as other forms of vision quest through fasting. The ways of the Pipe include orations that teach not only spiritual values, but also convey secular philosophies and social standards.

More vulnerable to attacks by non-Indians even than the ways of the Sacred Pipe are those of the Native American (Peyote) Church. Peyote rituals entered the Yankton's reservation through a small congregation east of Greenwood in about 1910. Peyote is a cactus plant that came into use as a religious sacrament among Indians of Mexico before Spaniards arrived during the 16th century. It was gradually adopted by members of tribes in the southwestern United States and moved up the Great Plains during the 19th century. Since then its use has spread to other areas across the United States and southern Canada. By the time Peyote reached Sioux Country about 1902, a substantial body of literature and documents denouncing it already existed. Sioux Peyote people are members of the Native American Church of North America.

A typical prayer meeting lasts from sundown to sunrise, and is followed by a ceremonial feast, a time for oration on community and cultural subjects, and social activities that extend into late afternoon. While singing and offering prayers through the night, each member ordinarily takes a small amount of peyote by chewing dried cactus (called buttons), by eating a mixture of ground peyote and water, or by drinking peyote tea. Joe Rockboy, after 65 years of experience, viewed Peyote to be a "part of creation" that served him as "a protector, a teacher, and a doctor." By consuming the herb while seated around the fire, he could receive for himself and others protection from physical harm, comfort through periods of crisis, healing for disease, and teaching on proper conduct in daily life.

The Sacred Herb is consumed as a sacrament, like the bread and wine of a Christian service. It is used not for its physical properties, but as a special gift from God with power to help an individual with a personal need. Hence, it is perceived to be a channel of communication with Grandfather God, thus holding a place in Indian religion similar to that of Jesus in Christianity. Federal officials classified it as a dangerous, hallucination-producing drug. Missionaries condemned it as an intoxicant like alcohol introduced by the devil. Neighboring non-Indians believed it caused addiction. Native American Church members deny any hint of hallucination, intoxication or drug-induced high, or addiction. Instead, they report an opportunity to reach out to the God of all religions. High standards of moral conduct preached by this group bear testimony to the truth of statements by its members. Federal officials in Washington, D.C., protect the use of peyote by Indians only as a religious freedom under the Constitution of the United States. Nevertheless, local federal officers, missionaries, and other critics have persecuted peyote users through legal action, social pressure, and ridicule. Occasionally, a high-ranking federal administrator has taken action against peyote users by charging them with such crimes as transporting a controlled substance through the mail and selling articles containing parts of animals that are protected by federal law.

Few have suffered greater abuse than Yanktons since the former tribal policeman Charlie Jones brought the herb to their reservation in 1910. Agency Superintendent Adelebert Leech placed Jones and several others in jail in 1912 and held them until As-

sistant U.S. Commissioner of Indian Affairs F. H. Abbott ordered their release. Abbott explained that the use of peyote was not an offense against any federal law. But subsequently Yanktons were harassed with threats of legal action, denial of equal opportunities in housing assignments, and discrimination in job placement. In the mid-1980s, several leaders of the Yankton Peyote group became victims of a sting operation ordered by U.S. Secretary of the Interior James Watt. Federal agents in Watt's employ came to the reservation, where only one in five employable persons held a job. Posing as collectors of artistic

Inside a tipi of the Native American Church, Neulan Dion (at left) watches roadman Asa Primeaux give an early birthday blessing to Chaska, the firstborn son of Clarence and Charon Asetoyer Rockboy.

objects, the agents offered substantial cash payments for religious paraphernalia that contained eagle feathers, wings, and claws. Possession of such items by Indians for religious purposes was legal, but selling products made with eagle parts was prohibited. Several Yanktons were convicted and sentenced to prison terms, even though they had been entrapped by federal agents who took advantage of their obvious need for cash to buy necessities for their families. Every victim of the sting believed it to be more an attack against their religion by a Christian fundamentalist than an effort to prevent the commercial sale of eagle parts.

The Yankton group has assembled with assurance of legal protection for more than a half century. For the first 12 years after the introduction of Peyote, believers held meetings secretly at homes on scattered allotments. In the autumn of 1922, however, they gained liberty to hold prayer meetings openly when state officials issued a corporation charter to the Native American Church of South Dakota. On November 28, Yanktons received approval for separate articles of incorporation under the name Native American Church of Charles Mix County. Soon afterward a family that had belonged to the group from the start donated a tract of land including an allotment house approximately one mile northeast of Greenwood. Here the congregation has maintained its religious home and burial ground. Members gather here regularly for prayers and often assemble elsewhere as well, meeting in tipis and homes on request by members in need of support. From this Yankton congregation, leaders have emerged to serve ably as officers in the incorporated Native American Church of South Dakota as well as in the organized Native American Church of North America.

Persecution has not stifled the Peyote religion or the benefits more than 100 Yanktons have gained from it. At homes in wintertime or in majestic tipis during warm seasons, they sit in a circle from sundown to sunrise to sing and pray as they meditate before the fire. After partaking of special food blessed beside the altar at sunrise, they spend the better part of a day sharing food and teaching cultural values. The way of Sacred Herb teaches strict moral conduct and abstention from the use of alcoholic beverages.

This way of worship does not exclude other forms. "There are three channels to the Great Spirit," explained the Yankton medicine man Charles Kills Enemy, "the Sacred Pipe, the Peyote, and the Cross." His ecumenical position is typical. Many Presbyterian, Episcopal, and Roman Catholic Yanktons participate in traditional Indian prayers. Together, the three religions make poverty conditions more tolerable as they perpetuate the traditions of the culture.

Religious practices of Indians take more time than do congregational activities of most non-Indian denominations, and they require a lot more commitment. Like reservation Chris-

A small group holds a noon feast after an all-night meeting of the Native American Church. Orations begin when the food distributed, and may last for several hours.

tian congregations, Greenwood Native American Church group members hold some scheduled prayer meetings—usually on the first Saturday of every month. Most ceremonies conducted the Pipe way, however, and prayer meetings of the Native American Church, take place on special request from a sponsor. A man or woman in need approaches a spiritual leader to ask for support from the group. The purpose may be to seek spiritual aid because of illness, financial need, chemical addiction, or almost any other problem. It may be to give thanks for good fortune, honor a relative, prepare for a vision quest, or any purpose that does not

abuse another person or dishonor the faith. If the medicine man of the Pipe way or the "roadman" of the Native American Church approves a request, the sponsor proceeds with full responsibility for preparations.

The preparations involve social obligations along with personal sacrifice. The sponsor supplies most of the religious paraphernalia required for a ceremony or prayer meeting. He or she extends invitations. Everyone invited is obliged to come if not prevented by a previous commitment or an illness. Thus all members of a group that prays the Pipe or Peyote way are under strong obligation to support every sponsor. In the Pipe way, preparations normally include the making of tobacco ties by the hundreds. To non-Indians they look something like a colorful rosary. To a sponsor, their preparation is an occasion for meditation.

At substantial cost, the sponsor acquires materials necessary to make the altar and provides the feast that follows the ceremony or prayer meeting. There must be plenty of food for every participant and a surplus for families to carry home. The cost may range from fifty or sixty to hundreds if not thousands of dollars for a single event.

The food is distinctly Indian, even though many ingredients now come from local groceries or supermarkets.

Since their early contacts with fur traders, Sioux people have been steady consumers of *Pejute Sapa*, or black medicine, known to non-Indians as coffee; this must be available in abundant supply. A guest at a Yankton feast will likely use disposable dishes and paper napkins and be served from commercial cookware. After ceremonies or prayer meetings sponsored to honor a relative or friend, the guest will surely take portions of the same types of decorated sheet cakes that Indians and non-Indians alike purchase from bakeries. Favorite treats include candy and gum, vats of Kool Aid, and tubs filled with iced bottles and cans of soft (never alcoholic) beverages.

After a prayer meeting, orations teach Yankton traditions to those who attend. The roadman speaks first. Others may speak only after he says, "Now I'm going to leave it open."

Prayer services of the Native American Church usually take place in a tipi, which holds 30 or more people. The 16 tipi poles are about 32 feet tall, and the interior diameter is about 30 feet.

Certain types of traditional food must be served too, prepared by women in ways that cannot be duplicated by non-Indian cooks. There is *wahanpi*, a soup containing generous quantities of meat and vegetables (if possible wild turnips and wild onions). There will be some kind of *wojapi*, a pudding made from canned berries or from wild fruit, such as buffalo berries, handpicked and preserved. There will be pans full of fry bread, dough fried in boiling lard. A religious feast ordinarily includes peppermint or some other variety of herbal tea.

Food service may take several hours, for everything that has been prepared must be distributed or given for participants to carry home. As the food distribution goes on, orations go on as well. Speakers announce coming events, report developments of interest to Indian Country, and pass along cultural information in stories and instructions. The feast ends only when each person with something to say has spoken, when the paraphernalia of worship have been put safely away, and after every scrap of paper has been picked up from the grounds.

(continued on page 89)

OBJECTS OF CEREMONY

The Yankton are Sioux in the middle, with habits, beliefs, and designs resembling those of Sioux people to both east and west. The flower designs in Yankton beadwork come from the tribes on the eastern prairies of Minnesota; the zigzag and triangular beaded designs are like those of the Tetons in the west.

Yanktons today observe traditional religions and celebrate special occasions in traditional ways. The clothing and accessories they wear at these events, and the objects they carry and use, represent their ultimate personal artistic expressions. Objects for ceremonies held in the ways of the Sacred Pipe or the Native American Church have symbolic as well as aesthetic appeal. Colors represent the six directions, concepts, and the spirit manifestations of living creatures. To Sioux people, for example, the color white calls to mind the north, thanksgiving, and white buffalo calf woman.

Like people everywhere, the Yankton continue to create beautiful objects just to be appreciated as well as for ceremonial use, even as they continue to appreciate and use objects made by their ancestors and handed down as family heirlooms. Quilts, drum beaters, feather fans, and other objects are valued not only in themselves but also for the occasions on which they have been used in the past.

Beaded bandolier bags, worn on festive occasions, might be hung on a wall for display at other times. This bag was made in the late 19th century by Minnie Whiteshirt, a Yankton. Beaded floral designs are sewn onto the velveteen front and shoulder straps of the bag, which is trimmed with ribbon and beaded yarn fringe.

Drumbeaters for Pipe ceremonies. **Top:** *Made by Yankton Francis Primeaux.* **Bottom:** *Made by a Lower Yanktonai woman and given to Teton head singer Buck Pomani on New Year's Day, 1967.*

Section of a beaded staff held by roadman at Peyote prayer meeting.

Star quilt in
traditional colors,
made especially to
be used while
fasting.

Medicine circles used
in the Yuwipi
ceremony. Only 3 or
4 inches across,
these are held by the
person who fasts.
The circle represents
the continuity of life
and the directions.
The color **black**
refers to healing.
Above: Colored
porcupine quills.
Below: Tiny cloth
pouches of tobacco
tied with string.

83

Rattles, made from gourds, are used to accompany singing at Peyote prayer meetings. **Left:** A water-bird gourd rattle trimmed with beads, given to the author by Joe Rockboy. **Right:** A gourd rattle that belonged to the Bruguier family, with a horsehair plume and braided hide fringe.

Quilt made by medicine woman Isabel Six Fingers Kills Enemy for the author's first fast, which was supervised by the quilt-maker's husband, medicine man Charles Kills Enemy.

Bead-trimmed moccasins are worn only for ceremonies and dances, not every day. *Top:* Fully beaded moccasins, geometric design, made in the late 19th century of early trade beads. *Bottom:* Partially beaded moccasins, flower design, early 20th century.

Feather fans are used in ceremonies to call on bird spirits and communicate with the fire. At Peyote prayer meetings, celebrants use the feathers of the road-man, or head singer, when they sing in turn. After midnight they take out their own feathers and other paraphernalia to enhance private prayer and medita-tion, a stunning sight that adds to the powerful experience. **Above:** *Two eagle-feather fans.*

Yankton women make exquisite star quilts for their families and friends for give-aways and personal gifts.

Top: *Hawk-feather fan used by author.* **Below:** *Bead-trimmed hair-tie for adolescent girl's coming-of-age cere-mony. She will keep her hair-tie to wear as part of her costume at dances and on other ceremonial occasions.*

Loom-beaded purse in western Sioux geometric design.

Sioux men wear spectacular medallions at ceremonies This one, of tiny beads in symbolic colors and trimmed with pipe beads and shells, shows the tipi that is a symbol of the Native American (Peyote) Church.

(continued from page 80)

Sometimes a give-away takes place while participants dine. This is a form of sacrifice offered by a sponsor on behalf of someone honored by the ceremony or prayer meeting. It is the appropriate way to honor a relative or friend who comes of age, for example, or has a birthday, or graduates from college. The sponsor prepares for many months—perhaps a year—often with help from relatives and friends. It is not unusual to see a family that lives on the edge of poverty distribute at a single give-away goods that would be worth more than $10,000 if they were sold in East Coast shops and galleries. A typ-ical give-away includes stacks of star quilts, numerous blankets, bead work of various kinds, and other items of aesthetic or practical worth according to what the sponsor believes an individual wants or needs. Every person in attendance must receive something—not less than a package of cigarettes or a wash cloth. The give-away shows sacrifice and respect. It is a tradition older than any printed record of Yankton customs. Despite a century of efforts to eliminate it as a practice contrary to mainstream capitalism, the give-away remains in use at major religious and social events on the reservation.

Family members celebrate a high-school graduation with a feast. The table at left displays desserts and gifts.

A give-away is an occasion for other expressions of generosity too. The person being honored receives attention as greeting cards are publicly read while food servers bring the gifts and decorated cakes to every guest for inspection. The sponsor stands at the center of the circle and addresses each participant with special words of appreciation. The person being honored at the ceremony also addresses each guest, and others who wish to make orations may do likewise. The gifts are only one of the ways of sharing that maintain the bonds of extended families and com-

Detail of lazy-stitch beading on tanned-hide wrist cuffs. Sioux women used the glass beads brought by European traders to decorate clothing worn for special occasions.

munities in a society attached to the reservation.

Sacrificial giving provides one of several outlets for the highest forms of art. An artist who produces an item for sale violates no code of ethics. Yet the most cherished items are made to be given away. Highest honor goes to the person who receives a star quilt, which Yankton women make so beautifully. Neither written records nor oral traditions trace this custom to its origin, but several things are clear. Quality blankets held special value for Yanktons as long ago as the fur-trade era. Private merchants and federal officials seeking favor with tribes provided goods that Indian people requested. At the top of every list of items desired in exchange for hides and pelts were many packages of Hudson's Bay or French blankets. Color preferences included natural and scarlet, and green or blue in several shades. After blankets, bolts of cloth were next on the list. The cloth was cut and sewn to form exquisite patchwork quilts featuring a multicolored star design. Favorite colors were those of symbolic religious importance—green, red, yellow, and white for the four directions, and blue for the eagle. Other colors may be added for aesthetic reasons or as a result of a vision.

Elders recall that, after federal officials rounded up ponies and guns near the end of the Sioux wars, high-quality blankets and colorful quilts replaced horses as major expressions of honor at give-aways. By the time a government-sponsored star-quilt industry opened on the Yankton Reservation in the 1930s, the art of quilt making and the act of quilt giving were already in place. They continue. None are finer than the star quilts produced by the Yankton women at Marty.

Crafting religious paraphernalia, jewelry, and other adornments from colored beads is also an important artistic expression. This too dates back to the fur-trade era. Every list of trade goods and federal annuities included quantities of beads in white, varying shades of blue and red, yellow, black, and clear glass. Beads came on strings of cotton thread, gathered in bunches, or hanks, according to color. Most hanks contained round, or seed, beads, and by midcentury traders introduced faceted cut-glass beads that glistened like diamonds in the sunlight. Since that time, Yanktons have excelled in the art of beadwork. None gives a better expression to this tradition than Clarence Rockboy. Every item he produces for sale is of superior quality. Each piece he makes as a gift or for use as a ceremonial instrument is a unique portrayal of culture as well as an exquisite expression of art.

Tied closely to religious and artistic traditions is music. Medicine man Charles Kills Enemy earned national recognition in the 1960s and 1970s as a

Clarence Rockboy creates beaded objects relating to the Native American Church. His work is prized for exemplifying both artistic and cultural values.

spiritual singer. Musicians of the Greenwood Native American Church are esteemed for their distinctive songs, especially for renditions of Peyote music in harmony. Yanktons are prominent performers at the big drum used for traditional powwow music.

There are powwow grounds in Lake Andes and Greenwood, as well as at Chouteau Creek Community Hall, established recently by families living in the east end of the reservation. Yank-

tons also conduct occasional *wacipis*, or dances, indoors throughout the year. Their dances do not gain as much attention as the international powwows held at Fort Totten and Rosebud. But each dance carries on an artistic tradition and is a major social event. Until the 1930s, wacipis held at seven dance halls were in direct competition with agency-sponsored fairs and festivals for the Yankton's attention. Today, enthusiastic attendance at powwows and wa-

Joe Rockboy, a lead singer at powwows and wacipis, *and one of the few Yanktons who recalled 19th-century rituals, played the powwow drum and taught traditional songs and dances.*

A wacipi, or dance, is held in the winter in the old armory of the University of South Dakota. Sponsored by the Yankton, it attracted many young people wearing elaborate dance costumes.

cipis reflects the cultural revival in evidence since the 1960s.

Yanktons are famed in Sioux Country for their contributions to oral literature. The late anthropologist Ella C. Deloria and Episcopal Father Vine Deloria, Sr. (both grandchildren of appointed Chief Francis Deloria) have been prominent contributors. The late "Grandma" White Tallow and Joseph Rockboy stood out among those who carried ancient legacies into the 20th century. The art of storytelling by these elders is an equivalent to any narrative composition by non-Indian authors. No Sioux tribe has a richer literary tradition than this.

Small wonder that Yankton people spend so little time on frills around the yards of their modest homes. Artistic beauty and cultural meaning find expression in so many other ways. Conspicuous consumption is frowned upon in tribal culture to a degree that most non-Indians cannot understand. For Yanktons, personal wealth has no relevance as the symbol of success. Instead, humility before God and sacrifice on behalf of community are their most prominent values. ▲

Leonard Bruguier is both a traditionalist and a scholar, specializing in the history of the Yankton Sioux. He is descended from the French trader Theophile Bruguier and the Yankton chief War Eagle.

THE
YANKTONS
TODAY

Today more than half of all Yankton people live in urban areas most of the time, mainly in four cities in South Dakota and Iowa. Some shuttle back and forth, living part-time in an urban world and part-time on the reservation. Their oldest urban centers are Sioux City of Iowa and Yankton city in South Dakota. These cities originated as band villages of the last two head chiefs, War Eagle and Struck-by-the-Ree. In Yankton city live approximately 750 Indian people, most of whom are either Yanktons or married to Yanktons. Some families have lived there for generations. Most live in a lowland community in the older part of Yankton around Picotte and Burleigh streets. In this city, tribal members have long endured prejudicial treatment enforced through custom. Few restaurants or other places of entertainment welcome Indian people. Jobs are available to them mainly at Gurney's Garden Seed and Nursery, a box factory, the state hospital, and one or two small business establishments.

Some tend the yards and gardens in a more prosperous area of the city, where they cannot take part in the social life. Most of those who are Christian affiliate with Christ Church Episcopal, which has attracted Indians since the days of Bishop Hare. Understandably, many drive across Chouteau Creek some 40 miles away for frequent participation in tribal activities on the reservation.

Sioux City contains more than 2,500 Indians representing a variety of tribes. These people live primarily in an area on the north side and experience significant job discrimination.

Yanktons who live in Rapid City, South Dakota, are more detached by distance and even more restricted by prejudicial customs. Two major housing developments form the core of an Indian community on the north side with a population that sometimes approaches 7,000. Most are Tetons. City officials ceded the initial tract of land for settlement by Indians who moved there to work on the construction of the

In Yankton city, Yankton Sioux people live in older homes like this one.

army air corps base during World War II. In return, Rapid City acquired federal property that had historically been used as an Indian boarding school. City leaders gave up another tract adjacent to the original neighborhood after a major flood swept Indian homes from a lowland close to the business district early in the 1970s, and they sought federal aid for the construction of new housing. Like those of Yankton city, Indians of Rapid City put up with uncomfortable and sometimes abusive treatment in exchange for job opportunities and educational benefits.

Harder to find are the more than 2,200 Indian people of Sioux Falls, where a number of Yanktons live full or part-time. No neighborhood concentration of Indians is readily identified by the more than 100,000 non-Indian inhabitants. Tribal members tend to meet at the Indian Center on the north side near the city center, but they live in housing scattered across the city. Some rent homes subsidized by public funds. Some live in apartment houses. Others rent units in trailer courts.

The life story of Leonard Bruguier illustrates why tribal members tolerate the hardships of urban life. Descended both from War Eagle and the French-Canadian trader Theophile Bruguier (cofounders of the community that evolved into Sioux City), he grew up in a family known well for its bicultural activities. A concerned mother took him from the reservation to Yankton city to take advantage of the better educational opportunities there. As he walked to school every day, he heard people calling out "little chocolate boy" when he passed their homes. He earned spending money by mowing lawns for the city's upper class. Peers cheered him as a superior athlete, and the librarian and a priest knew him as an accomplished student who spent countless hours at his books. But he was never accepted into the non-Indian society of his classmates; he could not attend their dances and parties. Leonard's daily life was typically segregated. Even though he dealt with non-Indians in the classroom and on the baseball diamond, he socialized only with other Indians. He served at the altar of Christ Church Episcopal and traveled often to the reservation, where he attended prayer meetings of the Native American Church and participated in ball games as well as social events.

After graduating from Yankton High School, Leonard went into combat with the marines in Vietnam. From there he went to the Pacific Northwest to work as a machinist. After nearly a decade, concern about extended separation from his cultural roots brought him home.

Curiosity inspired him to enroll at the University of South Dakota, where he earned a baccalaureate degree in history and a master of public administra-
tion degree. To support himself while at the university, he tended the gardens and grounds of a city park and coached the Little League baseball program in the area. He also served as assistant director of the South Dakota Oral History Center and investigated, for a federal agency, historical places related to the history of his tribe. In 1986 he entered a graduate program in history at Oklahoma State University, hoping to find academic employment near the Yankton reservation after earning a doctoral degree.

To be sure, this man would be outstanding in any group for his unusual achievements and personal popularity, but he is like other relocated Yankton people in important ways. Leonard accepts integration in urban life in return for educational and career opportunities and other benefits. Yet he retains his close attachment to the reservation because it is home, it serves as a retreat, and it sustains the traditions by which he lives.

Because the reservation is so important for tribal members from urban communities as well as those who live there full-time, political leaders of the tribe continue to search for ways to make it a viable place to live and work. Not discouraged by the failure of Father Fahsing's electronics plant at Greenwood and the tribal pork plant at Wagner, they hope to expand employment opportunities. Two new industries provide some jobs on the reservation today. One is a ranch on which Yankton people work at salary producing hay that is transported to distant markets. A truck carrying the hay is usually driven by beadwork artist Clarence Rockboy.

Another important industry is the Yankton Sioux Tribal Bingo Hall. Early in the 1980s, tribal leaders accepted help from investors in Kansas City to start this enterprise at an abandoned radar station in the Missouri Hills above Fort Randall Dam. At first, an unmarked sedan licensed out-of-state came frequently to collect 60 percent of the gross income, leaving only 40 percent for operating costs and profit to the tribe. After the investors recovered their initial contribution plus a considerable return, Yankton leaders took over the operation.

Now tribal members operate the bingo hall three days a week year-round. Alcoholic beverages and abusive conduct are prohibited. Customers drive in from miles around or ride a tribal bus that leaves from Sioux Falls and Fort Thompson. A food concession and the hall of game tables are filled most of the time. A large percentage of the patrons are older non-Indian women and men who regard this as a secure and pleasant place where one is likely to spend no more than forty dollars for a meal and an afternoon or evening of entertainment. They are a faithful clientele: A woman from Nebraska won the annual star-quilt award for 1986 for perfect attendance. She complained only once, after driving to the bingo hall in a blizzard and finding that it was closed. The bingo hall sup-

ports several reservation families at respectable levels of income.

Other employment on the reservation includes work on housing developments or other tribal projects, as funds become available. Some Yanktons are employed at the Wagner Public Health Service Hospital. Others commute to live and work off the reservation part-time.

When all the facilities of Marty Mission except the church and rectory were given to the tribe in the mid-1970s, tribal headquarters moved there from Greenwood. Officials occupy a building constructed in the 1950s as St. Sylvester's Convent. Two recently built housing units, along with the older homes on the mission grounds, comprise a small urban center. There are a high school boarding facility and a junior college that enroll mainly Indians. These are run by an Indian school board, and feature Indian values in a facility that Father Sylvester built to teach non-Indian ways.

St. Paul's Church at Marty illustrates the creative juxtaposition of Indian and non-Indian ways. It remains under the control of Benedictine priests from Blue Cloud Abbey and sisters of the Oblate Order of the Blessed Sacrament. Devout Yankton people come here for mass and instruction. Seniors from the Indian boarding high school come to the sanctuary for their graduation exercises. Various groups use St. Paul's for social and educational events. During a recent ecumenical conference, for instance, Charles Kills Enemy took the

Sacrament at Catholic mass on the same weekend that he conducted an Inipi ceremony in a sweatlodge within the mission compound. At the same conference, a non-Indian Jesuit priest, Father Paul Steinmetz, who had served mass, also entered a tipi near Lake Andes to participate in a Peyote prayer meeting as a singer. His mass was a Christian liturgy written in Sioux language and performed with Indian drumbeat accompaniment. It honored both Christ and the ways of the Sacred Pipe. The very appearance of St. Paul's epitomizes its bicultural nature. All figures shown in the stained glass windows are Indian, except for the image of Father Sylvester, the founder of Marty Mission, which was added to honor him after his death. The Virgin

St. Paul's Catholic Church was completed in 1946. The rectory is at the right. In his 28 years on the Yankton reservation, Father Sylvester built a major mission complex at Marty. He called his church "The Queen of the Prairie."

St. Paul's Catholic Church, in Benedictine style, was built of granite from Indiana. All the figures in the brightly painted choir of angels are Indian.

Mary and baby Jesus as well as a choir of angels above the altar are Indian. Designs in the vaulting above the sanctuary are Sioux. In its appearance and function, the entire church represents a deliberate and respectful blend of beliefs, customs, and values of both Indian and non-Indian people.

The appearance of the reservation's Protestant churches, which were constructed earlier, do not show the same respect for Indianness. Their founders lived at a time when cultural toleration was very limited. Although the Pres-

byterian John P. Williamson understood Yankton ways with greater depth than any other non-Indian missionary who served among the Sioux, he regarded the Sacred Pipe as an instrument of the devil. He was intolerant of give-aways, powwows, and other tribal practices. Although the Episcopalian Joseph Cook labored sincerely to fit into Yankton society, he similarly rejected the possibility of merging cultural values. Only a mixed-blood (whom he called a "half tone") could join his choir at Holy Fellowship Church in Greenwood. Father Cook required visible signs of change from those he allowed to become leaders in his churches.

Although Williamson and Cook allowed no compromise in church design, they gave control of their central and satellite churches over to Indians who made adjustments with apparent approval throughout the tribe. Protestant churches under Yankton leadership stand in isolated places where they are exposed to vandalism. Yet they are in excellent condition, showing no signs of damage, and are used regularly. On Sundays, members hold services in Sioux language and pray to God through a Christ who blends into Yankton philosophies. Some members pray also with the Pipe or Peyote and sense no violation of Christian belief.

Buildings constructed for secular uses show the same signs of adjustment. Those that the Yanktons never accepted are in disrepair. For example, only scattered foundations, two frame cabins, and a group of abandoned chalk-rock buildings remain from colonies that John Collier ordered, but Yankton people rejected. An entire complex of tribal facilities at Greenwood, constructed at federal expense to please administrators, is in ruin. Near Lake Andes, however, a remodeled farmstead houses the Yankton Sioux Tribal Alcoholism Program, with a sweatlodge on the grounds. A few miles away, on one tract of Indian land, stands a modern home with an expensive television dish antenna in the yard. On another, a tidy house stands next to a tipi of the Native American Church.

Each tribal member makes an individual choice about combining Indian and non-Indian aspects of life. Some Yanktons speak Sioux as a first language, pray mainly with the Pipe and Peyote, sponsor give-aways, send their children to predominantly Indian boarding schools, participate in powwows, and maintain close ties with their *tiospaye* (extended family group). But many do few, if any, of these things at their homes far away. Some may think of themselves as Indians only when they receive communications or payments due them from tribal officials. Others—such as the late Joseph Rockboy, his son Clarence, and Leonard Bruguier—have chosen to live active lives in both societies.

The varied responses of Yankton people after two centuries of contact with non-Indians under federal supervision represent those of Indian people across Sioux Country. At the east end, Minnesota Sioux endure the greatest pressure to accommodate to urban non-Indian society. Descendants of Mdewakantons and Wahpekutes at Prairie Island, for example, are threatened in many ways by the city of Red Wing. Some pray at a sweatlodge maintained by a former tribal chairman. Others share in Peyote meetings on the reservation. They have a powwow ground and a community hall. Prairie Island Sioux operate a profitable bingo hall. But from their homes, reservation residents look out to see vapor rising from vats near an atomic energy power plant. They commute to work in Hastings, Minneapolis, or St. Paul. They survive as a community of Sioux that carries on tribal traditions, but they do so under great stress from exposure to the life-style of urban non-Indians.

Out west on Pine Ridge, Cheyenne River. and Standing Rock reservations, people mainly of Teton and Yanktonai heritage endure less pressure from non-Indians and preserve the ways of their heritage in the most traditional forms. More isolated from non-Indian urban centers, they can more freely choose how to mix Indian with non-Indian ways.

Yankton life may be taken as one representative of tribal existence across 26 Sioux reservations. Reactions to their ways by non-Indian neighbors is fairly typical, too. Most non-Indian people in the region retain many of their own old country ethnic customs, for they belong to communities founded by immigrants little more than a century ago. In South Dakota, farmers of Czech heritage assemble at Tabor, east of Wagner, for Catholic mass on Sundays and for Czech Days every summer. In this they remain a group apart, because most non-Indian South Dakotans are Protestants of northern European heritage. An estimated 10 percent of the whole population uses German as a first or second language. Along the James River valley live Hutterites in communes governed by customs established in Europe during the Middle Ages. They are criticized and ridiculed

by their neighbors. Elsewhere, there are unique communities of Norwegians, Irish, Danes, Dutch, and other European nationalities. The isolation of each of the ethnic groups makes their members somewhat self-conscious and intolerant of the customs of other groups. All the ethnic groups of European origin, however, seem united in believing that the Sioux have the most unusual customs, should not be considered for marriage, and ought to be kept at some social distance.

In part, the racism on both sides reflects a tendency by all groups to look down on and exclude outsiders. To a large extent it is a holdover from the years in which it was the official policy of the United States to change the ways of Indians and to dissolve their tribes. Some degree of ignorance and fear from the Sioux wars of a century ago lingers still.

After a century, however, gradual change is apparent. The majority of non-Indians in the region now realizes that tribes and reservations are not likely to vanish. Younger people express curiosity and interest, albeit from a distance. A few non-Indians seek to become personally involved in Sioux activities, believing that all cultural interactions will improve human relations.

Recently, a majority of South Dakota legislators expressed a similar belief. They enacted a state law requiring that all teachers certified to work in public classrooms be trained in Indian

St. Philip the Deacon at Lake Andes, a satellite Episcopal church, has been restored to excellent condition. Members of the Deloria family, which includes outstanding cultural specialists and authors, are among the Yanktons buried in the cemetery here.

studies. Future teachers come to college courses on Indian history and culture with a reluctance they learned at home. As a result of these courses, some find the biases learned in their childhood to be unacceptable.

Privately, many Sioux and non-Indian people continue to express suspicion and resentment toward each other. But collectively, they are increasingly able to share ideas as neighbors who coexist in the same region. ▲

BIBLIOGRAPHY

Cash, Joseph H., and Herbert T. Hoover. *To Be an Indian.* New York: Holt, Rinehart and Winston, 1971. Excerpts from personal interviews preserved by the Oral History Center at the University of South Dakota express a view of tribal members regarding Sioux history and cultural traditions.

Deloria, Vine, Jr. *Custer Died for Your Sins: An Indian Manifesto.* New York: Macmillan, 1970. A great-grandson of the Yankton tribal band chief Francis Deloria wrote an emotional appeal for the better treatment of Indian people in an era of protest.

Hoover, Herbert T. *The Sioux: A Critical Bibliography.* Bloomington: Indiana University Press, 1979. Written for educators and general readers, this recommends approximately 200 books and articles that best describe the historical experiences and cultures of Sioux people.

Howard, James Heni. *The Dakota or Sioux Indians.* Vermillion, SD: Dakota Museum, 1966. An anthropologist explained Yankton and other Sioux tribal cultures as they were when first described by outsiders.

Marken, Jack W., and Herbert T. Hoover. *Bibliography of the Sioux.* Metuchen, NJ: The Scarecrow Press, 1980. Lists more than 3,300 published sources on Sioux history and cultures.

Sansom-Flood, Renee. *Lessons from Chouteau Creek.* Sioux Falls, SD: Augustana College Center for Western Studies, 1986. Tribal recollections of the years following the establishment of the Yankton's agency at Greenwood in 1859.

————, and Shirley A. Bernie. *Remember Your Relatives: Yankton Sioux Images, 1851 to 1904.* Marty, SD: Marty Indian School, 1985. Thirteen biographies with photographs illustrate the high quality of leadership in Yankton tribal history.

THE YANKTON SIOUX AT A GLANCE

TRIBE   *Yankton or Ihanktonwan*

CULTURE AREA   *Siouan; Great Plains*

GEOGRAPHY   *historically, the prairie from Mille Lacs Lake (Minnesota) to the Missouri River; currently a reservation in Charles Mix County, South Dakota. 1987 reservation land base (in approximate acres): 15,000 tribal + 22,000 allotment = 37,000 total.*

LINGUISTIC FAMILY   *Middle Sioux*

CURRENT POPULATION   *1987 tribal roll (approximate) includes: 2,980 on-reservation + 2,300 off-reservation = 5,280 total.*

FIRST CONTACT   *French trader-explorer Pierre Charles LeSueur, 1700. (Sioux first mentioned by Jean Nicolet ca. 1640; Middle Sioux including Yanktons first mentioned 1683.)*

FEDERAL STATUS   *recognized tribe. Yanktons are scattered (as a result of intermarriage, employment or educational opportunities, and other causes) on most Sioux reservations and in urban communities across the United States. On-reservation Sioux people recognized by the United States live mainly on four reservations in southern Minnesota (a fifth near Wabasha, called* Tipiota *by Sioux, closed in 1946), one in Nebraska, ten in South and North Dakota, and one in Montana. On-reservation Sioux people recognized by the Dominion of Canada live mainly on eight reserves in Manitoba and Saskatchewan. (Turtle Mountain and Cypress Hills communities established by Sitting Bull lost identity as reservation groups with Dominion recognition by the year 1910.)*

agricultural fair From the early 1890s to the mid-1930s, agencies in Sioux Country sponsored fairs to replace powwows, give-aways, and religious ceremonies as well as to uphold farming as a way of life.

allotment U.S. policy, applied nationwide from 1887, to break up tribally owned reservations by assigning individual farms and ranches to Indians. Intended as much to discourage traditional communal activities as to encourage private farming and assimilate Indians into mainstream American life.

annuities Based on terms of treaties or other agreements between the United States and individual tribes, annuities consisted of goods, services, and cash given to the tribe for a specified period (an average of 50 years for the Sioux).

Civilian Conservation Corps-Indian Department (CCC-ID) A 1930s program to provide conservation jobs for young men from reservations who would live in tent camps near their work and send home some of their wages.

cluster housing From the period of tipi villages to the present, some Yankton people have lived in groups and communities. Federal officials provided contemporary housing to accommodate this tendency in the 1930s, and again in the 1970s and 1980s on the Yankton Reservation. See also **scatter housing**.

The End of the Trail The place near Greenwood on the Yankton reservation where Yankton leaders decided to be the only Sioux tribe that would never officially take up arms against the United States.

fasting (hanble ceya) Seeking a vision by depriving oneself of food and water at an isolated place. Fasting may be carried on in seven different ways, the most rigorous of which is the Sun Dance.

fee patent The right to hold land as personal property, without restriction; land ownership.

give-away A Sioux tradition of personal sacrifice and sharing, to which federal officials and missionaries objected because it undermined adjustment to practices of free enterprise and personal saving.

Indian time The management of time to include traditional Indian commitments, which often conflict with work schedules of mainstream society and sometimes lead to loss of a job.

inipi The religious ceremony conducted in the Sioux sweatlodge.

Inkpaduta A leader of the militant protest against non-Indian immigration into eastern Sioux Country in the late 1850s, which killed some settlers in the Spirit Lake Massacre. He was never caught; some say he died of natural causes on the Fort Peck reservation.

issue-house The small, prefabricated house issued to tribal members from the early 1890s to about 1912 to encourage them to live on their allotment farms.

lawanpi The principal traditional ceremony, a song service, held in a tipi or home and conducted in the ways of the Sacred Pipe.

lower bands Communities that settled along the Missouri River on the east end of the Yankton reservation, led by Mad Bull, Struck-by-the-Ree, and other band chiefs, who encouraged them to cooperate with federal policies and goals.

medicine man or *woman* Spiritual leader in a congregation of the Sacred Pipe; may guide the person who fasts and conduct sweatlodge and other ceremonies.

Mitakuyase Literally "all my relatives"; a prayer recalling relations past and present and fulfilling the call to participate in the prayer circle of the Sacred Pipe; also used in place of the non-Indian "Amen."

Native American Church Of the three North American Indian Peyote religious organizations, the one to which Sioux Peyote congregations belong.

oration A traditional, semiformal means of transmitting cultural information during ceremonies, powwows and other events.

Peyote A cactus plant native to Texas, New Mexico, Arizona, and the northern Mexican states; used as the vehicle or channel of prayer in the Native American Church.

powwow A set of social activities, including a *wacipi* or dance. A wacipi may be held indoors in the winter, but a powwow is held out of doors in summer.

relocation Historical U.S. policy that attempted to move Indian people from a tribal environment into mainstream society. This policy was carried out in the 1950s and 1960s under the Voluntary Relocation Program and the Employment Assistance Program.

roadman The person who runs the prayer meeting in the Native American Church.

Sacred Pipe The symbolic channel to **Wakantanka** in traditional Sioux religion, made of stone from Pipestone Quarry.

scatter housing Traditionally, Sioux people lived in tipis at scattered locations when hunting or gathering food from natural sources. When they took allotments, they also lived at scattered locations, although in more permanent housing. Some still do so, while others prefer to live in cluster housing units on the reservation.

Sioux federation An alliance of 14 tribes of related heritage, culture, and dialects; also called the Sioux Nation.

soldiers' lodge Residence of young Yankton men who traditionally served as police in camps, leaders on hunting expeditions, and providers for the elderly. In the early reservation years, Struck-by-the-Ree organized the young men into the Grass Society to care for the elderly.

sponsor The person who was responsible for a traditional religious or social event. Such activities took place at the request of a sponsor and not on schedule as in non-Indian society.

surplus land Any land within reservation boundaries that was left over after allotment was considered to be surplus and could be purchased by Indians or sold to non-Indians on behalf of a tribe by federal officials.

sweatlodge The place where *inipi* ceremonies are held in the religion of the Sacred Pipe.

trust patent Under the General Allotment Act of 1887, the first allotments of land given out had trust status, controlled by the federal government on behalf of the Indians, who were not yet permitted direct ownership. The secretary of the interior supervised the use of trust land until a fee patent, permitting unrestricted use or sale, was issued to the Indian owner.

U.S. Farmer An individual who served as subagent while teaching non-Indian agriculture techniques and life-styles. Until the 1930s, he was the most influential official in a reservation community.

upper bands Bands in the northwest of the Yankton Reservation, especially communities led by Feather-in-His-Ear and other traditionalists, which resisted adaptation to non-Indian ways.

wacipi Literally means "they dance." See also powwow.

wahanpi Soup prepared for religious feasts and social occasions.

Wakantanka Tunkasina Literally means "God Grandfather"; suggests one's relationship through Mother Earth to the creator. God is not the father but the grandfather of human beings.

wojapi Berry pudding prepared for religious feasts and social occasions.

Yankton Delta or *Triangle* Names used in the 1850s to identify more than 11,000,000 acres between the Big Sioux and Missouri rivers, which were coveted by non-Indian settlers and made available to them by the Treaty of Washington, 1858.

yuwipi A ceremony of the Sacred Pipe religion that requires special vision and has particular use in healing.

ACKNOWLEDGMENTS

Four major contributors of Yankton heritage stand out: Joseph Rockboy, who shared the experiences of his life, which spanned the period from 1903 to 1982; Clarence Rockboy, Joe's son and a cultural specialist of high reputation; Leonard Bruguier, the grandson of Joe (in the Indian way); and the late Charles Kills Enemy, a renowned singer and medicineman whose name on the Yankton tribal roll years ago was Jonas Chasing Crane.

Substantial support for research came from the National Endowment for the Humanities, 1978 to 1981; and Paul Putz, director of the South Dakota Historical Preservation Center, who sponsored research and photography of sites related to Yankton tribal history. Documentary evidence to support the narrative came mainly from the National Archives, the Federal Archive in Kansas City, the Minnesota Historical Society, and the I. D. Weeks Library at the University of South Dakota. Essential cooperation came from many members and leaders of the Yankton tribe, and helpful assistance was extended by Renee Sampson-Flood, author of several books on tribal leaders and traditions.

PICTURE CREDITS

American Museum of Natural History, page 30 *right*; Bruguier Collection, page 94; Denver Public Library Western Collection, page 52; Federal Archive, Kansas City, pages 53, 57, 58, 65; Hoover Collection, cover, pages 34, 35, 37, 43, 44, 47, 48, 51, 60, 64, 67, 68, 70, 74, 76, 78, 79, 80, 82 *top and bottom*, 82–83, 83, 84–85, 86, 86–87, 87, 88, 89, 91, 92, 93, 96, 99, 100, 103; Museum of the American Indian, Heye Foundation, pages 12, 24, 30 *left*, 32, 54, 62, 72; National Archives, page 38; New York Public Library Collection, page 17; Smithsonian Institution National Anthropological Archives, Bureau of American Ethnology Collection, page 31; State Historical Society of North Dakota, page 19; South Dakota State Historical Society, pages 27, 41; The Thomas Gilcrease Institute of American History and Art, Tulsa, Oklahoma, page 26; Walters Art Gallery, page 16; W. H. Over Museum, pages 23 (Morrow Collection), 81, 82 *center*, 84, 85, 88 *inset*, 90.

Maps (frontispiece, pages 21, 28, 29, 40, 46, 50) by Karolyn J. Hoover.

HERBERT T. HOOVER is a native of Sioux Country who holds B.A. and M.A. degrees from New Mexico State University and a Ph.D. in American frontier history from the University of Oklahoma. Since 1967, he has served as professor of history at the University of South Dakota, and has focused attention on state history as well as the history of Indian-white relations across Sioux Country. Mainly on these subjects, he has authored or coauthored 6 books, contributed chapters to 7 others, and published more than 40 articles.

LEONARD R. BRUGUIER is a Yankton tribal member who grew up with attachments to both Indian and non-Indian cultures. After graduating from high school in Yankton city, he served in combat with the Fifth Marines in Vietnam and worked as a machinist in the Pacific Northwest. Then he earned B.A. and Master of Public Administration degrees at the University of South Dakota. In 1986 he entered a doctoral program in history at Oklahoma State University and began work on the Great Sioux Agreement of 1889 as a dissertation subject.